English Revision 101
Junior Certificate
Higher Level

Poems

Base details - death - war

Thickness of ice - love

The song of the wandering - fantasy
argus

SHORTCUTS TO SUCCESS
English Revision for Junior Certificate Higher Level

Louise O'Reilly

GILL & MACMILLAN

Gill & Macmillan Ltd
Hume Avenue
Park West
Dublin 12
with associated companies throughout the world
www.gillmacmillan.ie

© Louise O'Reilly 2005
ISBN-13: 978 07171 3834 0
ISBN-10: 0 7171 3834 8

Colour reproduction by Typeform Repro Ltd, Dublin.
Print origination in Ireland by Carrigboy Typesetting Services, Co. Cork

*The paper used in this book is made from the wood pulp of managed forests. For every
tree felled, at least one tree is planted, thereby renewing natural resources.*

PHOTO CREDITS

For permission to reproduce photographs and other material, the author and publisher gratefully
acknowledge the following:

62, 64, 65, 66 © The Advertising Archive; 48BR © Bill Bachmann/Alamy; ArenaPal: 93 © Elliott
Franks; 91 © Keith Saunders; 68, 69 © Camera Press Ireland; 115 © Corbis; 48TL © French Picture
Library, 74B © Mario Tama/Getty Images; 46 © Hooke and McDonald; 48 TR, 48BL © Imagefile
Ireland; 47 Picture Ronan Lang/courtesy Irish Independent; 72 © Irish Times Images; 83 © 20th
Century Fox Television/Jones, Sam/The Kobal Collection; Lonely Planet Images: 52T © Jerry
Alexander; 52B © Anders Blomqvist; 53B © David Greedy; 53T © Richard I'Anson; 49 ©
Pacemaker Press International; 74T © Rex Features; 55 © RTÉ Stills Library; 78 © Martyn Tu rner

The author and publisher have made every effort to trace all copyright holders, but if any has
been inadvertently overlooked we would be pleased to make the necessary arrangements at the
first opportunity.

Contents

"Romeo and Juliet"

"Boy Kills Man"

"Poetry:" - ①

②

○ Article writing pg 44

Acknowledgments

The author and publishers are grateful to the following for permission to reproduce copyrighted material:

Extract from *Of Mice and Men* by John Steinbeck (Penguin, 2000) Copyright © John Steinbeck, 1937, 1965;

Extract from *The Princess Bride* by William Goldman published by Bloomsbury reproduced by kind permission of Bloomsbury;

Frank O'Connor, excerpts from 'First Confession' from *Collected Stories*. Copyright 1950 by Frank O'Connor. Reprinted with the permission of Writers House. LLC New York on behalf of the proprietor;

Educating Rita and *Our Day Out* by Willy Russell published by Methuen Publishing Limited reproduced by kind permission of the publisher;

Extract from *Letter to Daniel: Despatches from the Heart* by Fergal Keane (Penguin Books, London, 1996). Copyright Fergal Keane, 1996. Reproduced by permission of Penguin Books Ltd.;

Extract from *Death and Nightingales* by Eugene McCabe published by Secker and Warburg. Used by permission of The Random House Group Limited;

'A boy's own book' by Declan McCormack and 'Mine's a skinny latte, Dahling' by Nikki Cummins first published in *The Sunday Independent*, 4 April 2004, appear courtesy of the writers and *The Sunday Independent*;

Interview with Anthony Murnane and RTÉ schedules © RTÉ 2004. Reproduced by kind permission of the *RTÉ Guide*;

'Hero's welcome for homegrown Olympic winner' by Melanie Finn first published in *The Irish Independent* reproduced by kind permission of *The Irish Independent*;

'Clamping rage' by Róisín Ingle first published by *The Irish Times*, 25 May 2004, appears courtesy of *The Irish Times*;

'Pressure to be perfect: teens under the knife' by Louise Holden first published in *The Irish Times* reproduced by kind permission of *The Irish Times*;

'In reality it's curtains, let's go celebrate' by Gavin Lambe-Murphy and 'Stars breed stars on TV' by Brendan O'Connor first published in *The Sunday Independent*, 22 February 2004, appear courtesy of the writers and *The Sunday Independent*;

Extract from 'The Crazy Wall' by John B. Keane Copyright © John B. Keane. Reprinted by kind permission of Mercier Press Ltd. Cork;

'Poem for Lara, 10' by Michael Hartnett reproduced by kind permission of the author and The Gallery Press, Loughcrew, Oldcastle, County Meath, Ireland. From *Collected Poems* (2001);

'Space Shot' by Gareth Owen from *Collected Poems for Children* Copyright © Gareth Owen 2000 Reproduced by permission of the author c/o Rogers, Coleridge & White Ltd., 20 Powis Mews, London W11 1JN;

Extract from 'The Pupil' (adapted for 2004 State Examinations) by Caro Fraser, published by The Orion Publishing Group reproduced by kind permission of The Orion Publishing Group;

'Shhhhhhhhhh!' by Hugh Linehan, first published in *The Irish Times*, appears in edited form courtesy of *The Irish Times*;

Extract from *The Glass Menagerie* by T.S. Eliot published by Methuen Publishing Limited Copyright © 1945 renewed 1973 The University of the South reproduced by kind permission of Methuen;

'Preludes' by T.S. Eliot from *Collected Poems 1909–62* published by Methuen Publishing Ltd. Copyright © 1945, renewed 1973 The University of the South reproduced by kind permission of Methuen;

Extract from 'Fear' by Rhys Davies reproduced by kind permission of Parthian Books.

The author and publisher have made every effort to trace all copyright holders, but if any has been inadvertently overlooked we would be pleased to make the necessary arrangement at the first opportunity.

1
Reading

In the Junior Certificate English exam one of the key skills that is required is the ability to read carefully and accurately. On Paper 2, in the Drama, Poetry and Fiction sections, you are required to read an unseen extract and answer the questions that follow.

In the Reading section of Paper 1 you will also be asked to read an extract from a novel or article and answer the questions that follow. These questions will usually ask you about the piece to make sure that you have understood it, but you may also be asked about matters of style.

As with all the questions on both papers, careful reading of the extract is vital. You may also be asked to give your opinion on the author of the piece. Your answers must always be based fully on the piece. Do not go off on a tangent. Keep your answers focused on the questions asked and use quotations where necessary.

1. Read the passage at least twice to fully grasp what the author is saying.
2. Read the questions that follow and return to the passage to re-read it with these questions in mind.
3. Taking the first question, focus on what exactly is being asked. Underline key words or phrases in the question that should be the focus of your answer.
4. Return to the passage to find suitable quotations or support for your answer.
5. Write your answer, but be careful not to over-write. Keep in mind the amount of marks awarded to the question. A five-mark answer should only be a few sentences, whereas a twenty-mark answer should be several paragraphs.
6. Use the space given in the answerbook. Neatness and presentation make a good first impression. Don't have your answers cramped on top of each other. Allow yourself space in case you wish to return to an answer later on.

The Questions

There are several tasks that you may be asked to carry out in this section. You will be asked *comprehension* questions based on your close reading of the text. You will also be asked questions on *writing style,* such as the identification of key features of the writer's style and your analysis of these features. You may also be asked to write something based on the information given in the text, e.g. an advertisement based on information given.

COMPREHENSION

- The questions ask you to find specific pieces of information in the text, such as the type of person the author was, and whether the experience lived up to expectations.
- You may be asked to form an opinion based on the information given in the text. Your answer *must* be based on the passage, so don't give opinions that aren't based on fact. For example, the type of person the author is may be revealed throughout the text through his/her use of humour, the serious tone of the passage, the use of anecdotal evidence, the use of historical reference or the reliance on factual information.

Key characteristics

Observant	Biased	Opinionated
Humorous	Enthusiastic	Tolerant
Determined	Helpful	Judgemental
Hard-working	Concerned	Optimistic/Pessimistic

- Your answer should be based around key words with support from the passage to prove your point. For example, the writer is very *observant* as he gives us a list of all the details he remembers.
- You may be asked to rewrite key sentences in your own words. Read the section/paragraph in which the underlined words appear to make sure you understand the *context* of the sentence. Don't worry if you don't understand the exact meaning of the words in the sentence. Guess the meaning of the words based on the extract as a whole. What would make sense?

STYLE

The second type of question you may be asked is to identify key features of the writer's style in the passage. Read the passage through carefully before answering this question. There are certain things to look out for, but this list is not finite and you may identify features that are not included.

Features of style

- **Questioning**
  Does the writer use rhetorical questions to make a point? Does the writer address the reader directly through questions? This creates an intimate style of writing.

- **Imagery**
  Does the writer use lengthy descriptions of people or places? Or possibly a few well-chosen adjectives to capture a scene? Does the writer's choice of words create an atmosphere or mood?

- **Exclamation**
  Does the writer use exclamation marks to create a sense of excitement, or anticipation or suspense?

- **Repetition**
  Does the writer repeat key words or phrases to focus the reader's attention? Are certain words repeated to create an atmosphere of gloom, excitement or tragedy?

- **Syntax**
  Does the writer use varied sentence lengths and structure to keep the reader's attention? A long sentence followed by a short one for example.

- **Alliteration**
  Does the writer use words that begin with the same letter in the same sentence to create an atmosphere? For example, 'The dull damp dreary room . . .'

- **Factual information**
  Does the writer use factual information to support his/her points? This may include statistics or lists of examples.

- **Reference**
  Does the writer refer to other sources such as biblical reference or reference to ancient myths or legends? Does the writer refer to other literary texts, such as Oliver in the Dickens' classic, *Oliver Twist*, 'I couldn't help but ask for more.'

- **Comparison**
  Does the writer describe things by comparing them to something else? The writer may use *simile* by comparing one thing to something else using the words 'like' or 'as'. For example, 'he was as thick as a post'. A comparison without using the words 'like' or 'as', is called a *metaphor*. For example, 'she was a gem of a find'.

- **Irony**
  Where the writer says one thing but means or implies another.

- **Anecdotes**
  Short, amusing stories used by the writer to illustrate the point being made.

Exam Questions

Read carefully the following article (in edited form) by Carin C. Quinn and then answer the questions that follow.　　　　　*(Junior Certificate, 2002)*

The Jeaning of America – and the World

This is the story of a sturdy American symbol, which has now spread throughout most of the world. The symbol is not the dollar. It is not even Coca-Cola. It is a simple pair of pants called blue jeans. They have been around for a long time, and it seems they will outlive even the necktie.

This ubiquitous American symbol was the invention of a Bavarian-born Jew. His name was Levi Strauss. He was born in Bad Ocheim, Germany, in 1829, and during the European political turmoil of 1848 decided to take his chances in New York, to which his two brothers had already emigrated. Upon arrival, Levi soon found that his two brothers had exaggerated their tales of an easy life in the land of the main chance. They were landowners, they had told him; instead, he found them selling needles, thread, pots, pans, ribbon, yarn, scissors, and buttons to housewives. For two years he was a lowly peddler, hauling some 180 pounds of sundries door-to-door to eke out a marginal living. When a married sister in San Francisco offered to pay his way west in 1850, he jumped at the opportunity, taking with him bolts of canvas he hoped to sell for tenting.

It was the wrong kind of canvas for that purpose, But while talking with a miner, he learnt that pants – sturdy pants that would stand up to the rigours of digging – were almost impossible to find. Opportunity beckoned. On the spot, Strauss measured the man with a piece of string and, for six dollars in gold dust, had the canvas tailored into a pair of stiff but rugged pants. The miner was delighted with the result, word got around about 'those pants of Levi's' and Strauss was in business. The company has been in business ever since.

When Strauss ran out of canvas, he wrote to his two brothers to send more. He received instead a tough, brown cotton cloth made in Nimes, France – called *serge de Nimes* and swiftly shortened to 'denim' (the word 'jeans' derives from *Genes*, the French word for Genoa, where a similar cloth was produced). Almost from the first, Strauss had his cloth dyed the distinctive indigo that gave blue jeans their name, but it was not until the 1870s that he added the copper rivets which have long since become a company trademark. The rivets were the idea of a Nevada tailor, Jacob W. Davis, who added them to pacify a mean-tempered miner called Alkali Ike. Alkali, so the story goes, complained that the pockets of his jeans always tore when he stuffed them with ore samples and demanded that Davis do something about it. As a kind of joke, Davis took the pants to a blacksmith and had the pockets riveted; once again, the idea worked so well that word got around. In 1873 Strauss appropriated and patented the gimmick – and hired Davis as a regional manager.

The company went from strength to strength and today more than two hundred and fifty million items of Levi's clothing are sold every year – including more than eighty-three million pairs of riveted blue jeans. They have become through marketing, word of mouth, and demonstrable reliability, the common pants of America. The jeans have become a tradition, and along the way have acquired a history of their own – so much so that the company has opened a museum in San Francisco. There was, for example, the turn of the century trainman who replaced a faulty coupling with a pair of jeans; the Wyoming man who used his jeans as a tow rope to haul his car out of a ditch; the Californian who found several pairs in an abandoned mine, wore them, then discovered they were sixty-three years old and still as good as new and turned them over to the Smithsonian Institute as a tribute to their toughness. And then there was the particularly terrifying story of the careless construction worker who dangled fifty-two storeys above the street until rescued; his sole support the Levi's belt loop through which his rope was hooked.

QUESTIONS

Answer the following questions:

1. From your reading of the passage what sort of person do you think Levi Strauss was? (10)
2. Basing your answer on the information given in this passage, write the text of an advertisement for Levi jeans. (10)
3. How does the writer make the historical facts presented in this article entertaining? (20)

SAMPLE ANSWERS

> Key words supported by reference to the text

1. From the passage we know that Levi Strauss was an *extremely hard-working man*. He hauled '180 pounds of sundries door-to-door to eke out a marginal living'. The word 'eke' shows us that his life was difficult and that his survival was a struggle.

   Levi also seems to be a very *courageous man*. He leaves behind his home when he travelled to the states 'to take his chances in New York'. Again when his married sister offers him an opportunity to go west he jumps at the chance. He has no hesitation in trying something new.

   When he speaks to the miner and realises he has an opportunity put his canvas to another use, Levi reveals himself to be a *true entrepreneur*. He sees an opportunity and takes it. He is also not afraid to expand on his original idea and incorporates the ideas of others, such as the rivets used by Jacob Davis.

Advertisement

Look at the Media Studies section for ideas on the use of persuasive language and slogans. In this section answers should be based on the text.

---

2. *Levi Jeans*

   Established in 1850, Levi jeans are the corner stone of the American Wild West. Made to be rugged. Designed to withstand the extremes of the outdoors and riveted for strength.

   The jeans that will go on forever. When all else fails you can depend on your Levis to get you out of trouble: if you are hanging by your belt loop fifty-two storeys up or towing your car out of a ditch!

   Levi Jeans. Tradition and Strength.

3. The writer makes the historical facts in this article entertaining by showing us the *human side* of the characters involved. Levi Strauss was not a rich businessman but a poor émigré. He struggled to make a living in New York and eventually went out west. It is *amusing* to think that the reason why he was able to found his business was because he made a mistake and brought out the wrong type of canvas. His brothers then make a further mistake and that is why we call them denim jeans.

The writer keeps the reader's attention throughout the piece by varying the *syntax* and structure of her writing. The first paragraph consists of short concise sentences as it leads up to the beginning of Levi Strauss's story. This contrasts greatly with the second paragraph where the sentences are long and involved, to fill us in on all the details of his life.

The writer also uses *anecdotes* to illustrate her story. The *anecdote* of Jacob Davis riveting his customers trousers 'as a kind of joke' and then the idea catching on, brings the story to life.

The history of Levi jeans is finally summed up in the amusing stories of their disparate uses. Everything from saving a train to saving a man's life is credited to this amazing item of clothing.

Read carefully the following article in edited form by Cyril Kelly and then answer the questions.

Eating an Ice Cream Cone

It was a sweltering day and the sash-windows of our third class were opened as wide as possible to gulp any stray puff of fresh air. Outside, swallows were arcing like black bolts of voltage against the blue sky. Master McMahon had had to call on all his stamina and wizardry to keep forty of us on our collective mettle since early morning. But, as the minute hand of the clock ticked towards three, there was one delightful twist left in the day.

Pressing the blackboard firmly against the easel, he wrote the title of the story we were getting for homework, namely 'Eating an Ice Cream Cone'. Then turning to face us and, without uttering a word, he pushed up the white cuffs of his shirtsleeves as far as they would go. In the expectant hush, he slowly undid the strap of his rectangular watch and placed it on the table.

From that moment his stern eyes no longer needed to demand our attention. He had become a nine-year-old boy approaching the high windowsill of our classroom to buy a cone. Nobody in the class dared to blink, I hardly allowed myself to breathe. We saw him proffer his money up to some shopkeeper who must have been as gigantic as Fionn MacCumhaill. We were parched as we waited for him to be served.

Occasionally, the raucous call of a rook ripped the backdrop of silence which was the only prop for his performance.

As our mime artist turned away from the counter, we were entranced by his widening, expectant eyes. We salivated as, firstly, he licked his lips and then fastened a fond smile on his upheld fist. We, too, agonised on how to best tackle this cone which had materialised before our hungry eyes. Should he lick the quiff of soft ice cream that drooped with a cowlick at the apex, or should he tackle the fronds melting over the crisp edge of the cone?

Forever the *agent provocateur*[1] against predictability, he suddenly raised the ice cream, got his mouth under the golden tip and snipped off the plain bit at the end. The crumbling cone crackled in every inner ear and brought more water to our teeth and we watched as, manfully, he tried to suck the ice cream through the small opening in the end.

The other classes were on their noisy way out of the building but Master McMahon remained motionless, with his knees bent for balance, his head thrown back and his face upturned towards the ceiling. Frozen for a moment in that pose, he was the strong man in the circus, the base of the human pyramid, supporting the combined expectancy of forty spellbound boys. As he resumed sucking for ice cream, his cheeks grew more and more hollow. We could feel the ice cream offering stout resistance and we were craning forward on the edges of the benches, almost asphyxiated with anticipation, our cheeks also concave with phantom pain.

At last with a resounding pop, his cheeks relaxed and we new that he had, finally, sucked an air hole through the dense ball of ice cream. The relief in that classroom was audible. What an expression of Dennis the Menace satisfaction Master McMahon had on his face! As he put on his watch again and before we could stretch out of our trance, he pointed to the words on the board and said: 'Tomorrow I'll give the price of an ice cream to any boy who makes me taste the flavour of vanilla from his story.'

[1] One who provokes others into action

QUESTIONS

Answer the following **three** questions.
1. Master McMahon wants the boys to make him, 'taste the flavour of vanilla from his story'. What kind of writing is he trying to encourage from his pupils when he says this? Explain your answer.
2. The writer uses many attractive images in his writing. Pick out one that you particularly enjoyed and say why you liked it.
3. In this passage Cyril Kelly recalls an incident from his childhood. Do you think he is a good storyteller? Support your answer with reference to the text.

(Junior Certificate, 2003)

Personal Writing 2

In this section you have the opportunity to show off your writing skills in whatever format suits you best. There are eight or nine titles to choose from and most allow you to choose the format in which you wish to write, e.g. narrative, descriptive, dramatic, short story and so on. Regardless of what choice you make, you must ensure that you follow the guidelines given on the paper.

You will be rewarded for:

- A personal approach to the subject.
- An appropriate style.
- Liveliness and a good choice of words.
- Organisation and accuracy.

In each of these categories good spelling and punctuation are necessary

There are several types of compositions that you may be asked to write:

- Short story
- Descriptive essay
- Debate speech
- Dialogue
- Discursive essay
- Diary entry
- Letter

As this section of the exam is worth seventy marks, it is worth your while reading examples of each style and experimenting with writing in each of these styles to see which style suits you best. In each case, there are some basic points you should be aware of.

1. You should **plan** your essay first to prevent rambling and irrelevance.

2. Your essay should be divided into paragraphs. Each paragraph marks a transition to a new point or progression of plot.
3. Use words appropriate to the task set. For example, the informal language of a diary entry would not be suitable in a discursive essay or a formal letter.
4. Your spelling and grammar should be accurate, avoid obvious mistakes.

Your essay should have at least 8–12 paragraphs to allow for the good development of ideas. Depending on your writing size and style it should be 3–4 pages of your answerbook (A4).

Short Story

Some basic elements are common to all good short stories.

1. **Plot:** The story should focus on one or two events. You have a very limited time in which to write (one hour), so it is better to concentrate on one or two events and tell them well rather than to skim through a complex plot. **Obvious copying from films, television, novels etc. will be penalised.**

2. **Characters:** Your story should engage the reader so your characters should be well developed and not just a list of physical characteristics. If you are going to use some direct speech, make sure that it is correctly punctuated and interesting (see punctuation guide in last section). It should add something to the story by revealing aspects of the story to the reader. If it doesn't add to the story then leave it out.

3. **Relationships:** The interaction between the characters provides the story with depth and realism. Try to avoid stereotypes.

4. **Structure:** In general terms the story should have a beginning, middle and end. You may decide to alter this structure but the story should build to some type of climax using suspense to keep the attention of the reader.

5. **Setting:** The reader should get a sense of time and place from the opening section of your story. This can be created by references to the locality, descriptions of the scene, the clothing or dress of the characters. This will also create atmosphere and mood. Use adjectives to create a scene and add depth to your descriptions.

Bearing these points in mind read the short story and answer the questions that follow. The story is by Saki and is called *The Open Window*. It is reproduced here in edited form.

The Open Window

'My aunt will be down presently, Mr Nuttel,' said a very self-possessed young lady of fifteen; 'in the meantime you must try and put up with me.'

'I know how it will be,' his sister had said when he was preparing to migrate for a nerve cure to this rural retreat: 'you will bury yourself down there and not speak to a living soul, and your nerves will be worse than ever from moping. I shall just give you letters of introduction to all the people I know there. Some of them, as far as I can remember, were quite nice.'

Framton wondered whether Mrs Sappleton, the lady to whom he was presenting one of the letters of introduction, came into the nice division.

'Do you know many of the people round here?' asked the niece, when she judged that they had had sufficient silent communion.

'Hardly a soul,' said Framton. 'My sister was staying here, at the rectory, you know, some four years ago, and she gave me letters of introduction to some of the people here.'

'Then you know practically nothing about my aunt?' pursued the self-possessed young lady.

'Only her name and address,' admitted the caller.

'Her great tragedy happened just three years ago,' said the child; 'that would be since your sister's time.'

'Her tragedy?' asked Framton; somehow in this restful country spot tragedies seemed out of place.

'You may wonder why we keep that window wide open on a October afternoon,' said the niece, indicating a large French window that opened onto a lawn.

'It is quite warm for the time of year,' said Framton; 'but has that window got anything to do with the tragedy?'

'Out through that window, three years ago to a day, her husband and her two young brothers went off for their day's shooting. They never came back. In crossing the moor to their favourite snipe-shooting ground they were all three engulfed in a treacherous piece of bog. Their bodies were never recovered. That was the dreadful part of it.' Here the child's voice lost its self-possessed note and became falteringly human. 'Poor aunt always thinks that they will come back some day, they and the little brown spaniel that was lost with them, and walk in at that window just as they used to do. That is why the window is kept open every evening till it is quite dusk. Do you know, sometimes on still, quiet evenings like this, I almost get a creepy feeling that they will all walk in through that window —'

She broke off with a little shudder. It was a relief to Framton when the aunt bustled into the room with a whirl of apologies for being late in making her appearance.

'I hope Vera has been amusing you?' she said.

'She has been very interesting,' said Framton.

'I hope you don't mind the open window, said Mrs Sappleton briskly, 'my husband and brothers will be home directly from shooting, and they always come in this way.'

She rattled on cheerfully. He was conscious that his hostess was giving him only a fragment of her attention, and her eyes were constantly straying past him to the open window and the lawn beyond. It was certainly an unfortunate coincidence that he should have paid his visit on this tragic anniversary.

'The doctors agree in ordering me complete rest, an absence of mental excitement, and avoidance of anything in the nature of violent physical exercise,' announced Framton.

'No?' said Mrs Sappleton, in a voice which only replaced a yawn at the last moment. Then she suddenly brightened into alert attention – but not to what Framton was saying.

'Here they are at last!' she cried. 'Just in time for tea, and don't they look as if they were muddy up to the eyes!'

Framton shivered slightly and turned towards the niece with a look to convey sympathetic comprehension. The child was staring out through the open window with dazed horror in her eyes. In a chill shock of nameless fear, Framton swung round in his seat and looked in the same direction.

In the deepening twilight three figures were walking across the lawn towards the window; they all carried guns under their arms, and one of them was additionally burdened with a white coat hung over his shoulders. A tired brown spaniel kept close at their heels. Noiselessly they neared the house. Framton grabbed wildly at his stick and hat; the hall-door, the gravel-drive, and the front gate were dimly noted stages in his headlong retreat. A cyclist coming along the road had to run into the hedge to avoid imminent collision.

'Here we are, my dear,' said the bearer of the white mackintosh, coming in through the window; 'fairly muddy, but most of it's dry. Who was that who bolted out as we came up?'

'A most extraordinary man, a Mr Nuttel,' said Mrs Sappleton; 'could only talk about his illnesses, and dashed off without a word of good-bye or apology when you arrived. One would think he had seen a ghost.'

'I expect it was the spaniel,' said the niece calmly; 'he told me he had a horror of dogs. He was once hunted into a cemetery somewhere on the banks of the Ganges by a pack of pariah dogs, and had to spend the night in a newly dug grave with the creatures snarling and grinning and foaming just above him. Enough to make anyone lose their nerve.'

Romance at short notice was her speciality.

From the *The Open Window* by Saki

QUESTIONS

Look at the short story with the previous headings in mind.

1. What event is described?
2. Which characters are involved?
3. How are the characters depicted?
4. What is the relationship between the two central characters? How do they interact with each other?
5. Outline the plot in terms of beginning, middle and end.
6. How is the setting depicted?

GETTING STARTED

Step 1: The plan

Before you begin your story you **must** have a plan in mind. The lack of a plan results in rambling, unfocused stories and stereotypical endings. The usual sign of a badly planned story is the conclusion 'and then I woke up'. This usually indicates that the author had no idea where the story was going and so took the easy option of pretending it was all a dream.

There are several methods of planning an essay and you must find the one that suits you best. Regardless of method, the aim of a plan is to get all your ideas on paper, organise them into some semblance of order and structure the story that you will write.

The spider diagram

- The spider diagram method of planning an essay involves putting the title of the story in the middle of the page with a circle around it.
- You then jot down all the ideas you have around the outside of the circle.
- When you have exhausted your ideas you then begin to number the order you will put them into the story, possibly eliminating those you now find don't suit.
- You could add additional words or phrases to develop the ideas in the plan. You must decide the order the ideas will appear in; know the basic structure of the plot (beginning, middle and end); and choose the setting and the characters. Then you can begin writing your essay.

SAMPLE PLAN

Take for example the title 'Exploring'.

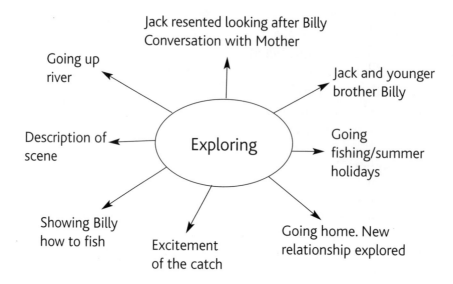

When you have jotted down your ideas and have an idea where the story is going, you can then number the points or group some together. Each number should become a paragraph within the story.

Step 2: *Writing the story*
The opening paragraph

The opening paragraph should capture the attention of the reader. Try to begin with a sentence that will lead the reader to read on. Don't reveal everything in the first paragraph. If you want to start the story with direct speech make sure it is punctuated properly (see punctuation section). Background information can be filled in throughout the story, it doesn't all need to be in the first sentence. Try to avoid beginning your story with sentences such as, 'Jack was ten. He had a brother who was seven. They lived in the countryside. It was the summer. They were going fishing but Jack didn't want to look after his brother.'

Use your imagination! Fill the story with adjectives that give the reader a sense of place and atmosphere. For example:

'The sun blazed down on that most precious of days, the last day of the summer holidays. There was a sense that every moment was sacred, as indeed it was, for from the following day all freedom was gone and most daylight hours would be spent in the confines of the classroom. Jack was trying to avoid his mother as he knew that looking after his little brother was high on her agenda of things for Jack to do. Jack had other plans.'

The body of the story

The body of the story should contain at least six or seven paragraphs. Allow your story to develop, don't rush to a conclusion. Take your time to describe the atmosphere of the scene and the feelings of the characters. Remember that there is more to describing a scene than just the physical aspects. Try to use more than one sense. Describe the sounds, tastes, smells and touch, as well as the sights of the scene. How the character feels gets the reader to engage with the text, so try to give an insight into how they respond to events in the story.

The climax or conclusion of the story should be planned. As the writer, you should know where the story is going, but the reader doesn't need to until the very end. Look at the story above to see how the writer twists the story in the final lines from a ghost story to a prank played by a young girl. Use suspense!

SAMPLE QUESTIONS

Write a short story based on one of the following titles. Remember to **plan** your story before you begin!

1. Your favourite team/pop group are playing one match/concert in Ireland, but you have failed to secure a ticket. Write the story of how you managed to attend the event anyway. (*Junior Certificate, 2002*)
2. A catastrophe (*Junior Certificate, 2001*)
3. You awake one night to find a small but friendly alien sitting at the foot of your bed. (*Junior Certificate, 1998*)
4. A family outing (*Junior Certificate, 1997*)
5. Exploring (*Junior Certificate, 1996*)

The Descriptive Essay

While similar to the short story, the descriptive essay focuses on describing a person, place or event. The aim of descriptive writing is to provide the reader with a vivid mental image of the topic discussed. There isn't the same sense of plot as in the short story; there may never be a climax in the essay, but that is not the point.

Writers use not only adjectives but also varying sentence length, anecdotes and examples to bring a scene to life.

The following text is an example of a piece of descriptive writing that sets the scene for the novel that follows.

Of Mice and Men

A few miles south of Soledad, the Salinas River drops in close to the hillside bank and runs deep and green. The water is warm too, for it has slipped twinkling over the yellow sands in the sunlight before reaching the narrow pool. On one side of the river the golden, foothill slopes curve up to the strong and rocky Gabilan mountains, but on the valley side the water is lined with trees – willows fresh and green with every spring, carrying in their lower leaf junctures the debris of the winter's flooding; and sycamores with mottled, white, recumbent limbs and branches that arch over the pool. On the sandy bank under the trees the leaves lie deep and so crisp that a lizard makes a great skittering if he runs among them. Rabbits come out of the brush to sit on the sand in the evening, and the damp flats are covered with the night tracks of 'coons, and with the split-wedge tracks of deer that come to drink in the dark.

There is a path through the willows and among the sycamores, a path beaten hard by boys coming down from the ranches to swim in the deep pool, and beaten hard by tramps who come wearily down from the highway in the evening to jungle-up near water. In front of the low horizontal limb of a giant sycamore there is an ash pile made by many fires; the limb is worn smooth by men who have sat on it.

Evening of a hot day started the little wind to moving among the leaves. The shade climbed up the hills toward the top. On the sand banks the rabbits sat as quietly as little, gray, sculptured stones. And then from the direction of the state highway came the sound of footsteps on crisp sycamore leaves. The rabbits hurried noiselessly for cover. A stilted heron laboured up into the air and pounded down river. For a moment the place was lifeless, and then two men emerged from the path and came into the opening by the green pool.

They had walked in single file down the path, and even in the open one stayed behind the other. Both were dressed in denim trousers and in denim coats with brass buttons. Both wore black, shapeless hats and both carried tight blanket rolls slung over their shoulders. The first man was small and quick, dark of face, with restless eyes and sharp, strong features. Every part of him was defined: small, strong hands, slender arms, a thin and bony nose. Behind him was his opposite, a huge man, shapeless of face, with large, pale eyes, with wide, sloping shoulders; and he walked heavily, dragging his feet a little, the way a bear drags his paws. His arms did not swing at his sides, but hung loosely.

From *Of Mice and Men* by John Steinbeck

QUESTIONS

1. How does the author establish a sense of place?

2. Which words or phrases does he use to describe nature in the passage? Are they positive images?
3. Which sounds are described?
4. Which other senses are used in the description of the scene?
5. How are the two men described?
6. What is implied about their personalities through the description of their clothes, actions and physical features?

As with the above passage, in the extract below characters are often described in terms of their actions. Sometimes the writer uses humour to express his opinion of a character. Read the passage below and examine how the writer gives the reader an impression of a character.

The Princess Bride

Prince Humperdinck was shaped like a barrel. His chest was a great barrel chest, his thighs mighty barrel thighs. He was not tall but he weighed close to 250 pounds, brick hard. He walked like a crab, side to side, and probably if he had wanted to be a ballet dancer, he would have been doomed to a miserable life of endless frustration. But he didn't want to be a ballet dancer. He wasn't in that much of a hurry to be king either. Even war, at which he excelled, took second place in his affections. Everything took second place in his affections.

Hunting was his love.

He made it a practice never to let a day go by without killing something. It didn't matter what. When he first grew dedicated, he killed only big things: elephants or pythons. But then, as his skills increased, he began to enjoy the suffering of little beasts too. He could happily spend an afternoon tracking a flying squirrel across forests or a rainbow trout down rivers. Once he was determined, once he focused on an object, the Prince was relentless. He never tired, never wavered, neither ate nor slept. It was death chess and he was international grand master.

From *The Princess Bride* by William Goldman

QUESTIONS

1. What impression do we get of the Prince from the above description?
2. What do you think is the author's opinion of the Prince?
3. Which images of the Prince give you this impression?

In addition to people and places, writers describe events by focusing on the reactions of the central character to the story as it unfolds. Read the following extract from a short story and examine the methods used by the writer to create a sense of immediacy and realism.

In this extract, Jack, accompanied by his tyrannical sister Nora, is about to complete his first confession. He has heard terrifying stories and, as he is quite young, is prepared for anything.

First Confession

It was pitch-dark and I couldn't see priest or anything else. Then I really began to be frightened. In the darkness it was a matter between God and me, and he had all the odds. He knew what my intentions were before I even started; I had no chance. All I had ever been told about confession got mixed up in my mind, and I knelt to one wall and said: 'Bless me, father, for I have sinned; this is my first confession.' I waited for a few minutes, but nothing happened, so I tried it on the other wall. Nothing happened there either. He had me spotted all right.

It must have been then that I noticed the shelf at about one height with my head. It was really a place for grown-up people to rest their elbows, but in my distracted state I thought it was probably the place you were supposed to kneel. Of course, it was on the high side and not very deep, but I was always good at climbing and managed to get up all right. Staying up was the trouble. There was room only for my knees, and nothing you could get a grip on but a sort of wooden moulding a bit above it. I held on to the moulding and repeated the words a little louder, and this time something happened all right. A slide was slammed back; a little light entered the box, and a man's voice said: 'Who's there?'

''Tis me, father,' I said for fear he mightn't see me and go away again. I couldn't see him at all. The place the voice came from was under the moulding, about level with my knees, so I took a good grip of the moulding and swung myself down till I saw the astonished face of a young priest looking up at me. He had to put his head on one side to see me, and I had to put mine on one side to see him, so we were more or less talking to one another upside-down. It struck me as a queer way of hearing confessions, but I didn't feel it my place to criticise.

'Bless me, father, for I have sinned; this is my first confession,' I rattled off all in one breath, and swung myself down the least shade more to make it easier for him.

'What are you doing up there?' He shouted in an angry voice, and the strain the politeness was putting on my hold of the moulding, and the shock of being addressed in such an uncivil tone were too much for me. I lost my grip, tumbled, and hit the door an unmerciful wallop before I found myself flat on my back in the middle of the aisle. The people who had been waiting stood up with their mouths open. The priest opened the door of the middle box and came out, pushing his biretta back from his forehead; he looked something terrible. Then Nora came scampering down the aisle.

'Oh, you dirty little caffler!' she said. 'I might have known you'd do it. I might have known you'd disgrace me. I can't leave you out of my sight for one minute.'

From 'First Confession' by Frank O'Connor

QUESTIONS

1. How do we know that the main character is quite young?
2. What senses does the main character use to describe his surroundings? Give examples.
3. What does Nora's reaction tell us about her personality?

As with the short story, you must plan your essay fully before you begin. Look at the various aspects of description: sights, sounds, smells, tastes, touch as well as atmosphere and response of the narrator to the situation.

Use the examples above to help you in your writing.

SAMPLE QUESTIONS

Write a descriptive essay based on one of the titles below.

1. Describe a place you love to visit. (*Junior Certficate, 2002*)
2. Write a lively account of your home place and its personalities as seen through the eyes of a total stranger on a visit there. (*Junior Certficate, 1999*)
3. My city/town at 2.00 a.m.

OR

The disco

OR

An autumn landscape (*Junior Certficate, 1998*)

4. Describe the experience of a visit to one of the following:
   (a) A street market
   (b) A fair or mart
   (c) A carnival or funfair

To evoke the experience graphically it may help if you bear in mind some of the following: the sights, sounds, tastes, smells and touches of the experience. (*Junior Certificate, 1996*)

Speech Writing

You may be asked to write a speech for a number of different occasions but the usual type of speech you will be asked to write is a debate speech on a particular motion. With a debate speech you are speaking as part of a team and you must support one side of the argument or the other. You may mention other parts of your team argument that you will not deal with in detail.

While writing a speech you must always be aware of the audience you are addressing. You must aim to capture their attention and keep it. There are a number of ways to do this that vary according to the type of speech you are writing.

INGREDIENTS OF A GOOD SPEECH

1. Opening statement

Usually a speech will begin with 'Ladies and Gentlemen'. If you are addressing a specified audience you should mention this in your opening statement. For example, 'Good evening ladies and gentlemen, classmates, teachers, Reverend Father and past-pupils. I would like to welcome you all to the official opening of the new school extension'.

In a debate speech the usual greeting is, 'Chairperson, adjudicators, members of the opposition/proposition, friends. We are here tonight to discuss the motion that . . . .'

2. Facts

From welcoming a visitor to debating the world debt crisis, the central plank of your speech should be *factually based*. Mention past events, present develop-ments and future plans that are relevant to the topic. As this is an English exam and not a court of law don't feel obliged to omit details because you are not sure that they are true. Facts take many different forms. You can use *statistics* to support your point, 'Sixty per cent of all junior cert. students spend three hours studying every night'. You can also use *reference*. You may refer to a poll carried out, reports, books/authors etc. 'According the recent OECD survey. . . .' 'Professor Martin of Trinity College has recently proven that . . . .' Another useful book to quote from is always the Bible. For example in a debate on world poverty you could quote what the Bible says that 'the poor will always be with us'. Or for the opposite side of the argument, the Bible says, 'it is easier for a camel to pass through the eye of a needle than for a rich man to enter the kingdom of heaven'.

3. Persuasive argument

Especially in the case of a debate speech, your aim is to convince the audience of the validity of your argument. There are several useful ways of trying to convince the audience that your proposal is correct.

- **Rhetorical question:** Ask a question to which the audience already knows the answer, e.g. 'Do we want a better healthcare system? Does the proposition want us to believe that we don't?'

- **Emotive language:** Try to engage the emotions of the audience in the argument you are trying to put forward, e.g. 'The life of every starving child in Africa is in your hands. It is up to you if they live or die.'
- **Triads:** Throughout well-written speeches you will find that the speaker has grouped their points into threes. These are called triads and add balance and clarity to your argument, e.g. 'What we need is hard work, determination and the will to succeed.' ' History can teach us what happened in the past, the causes of present strife but the future solutions are up to us.'
- **Repetition:** This is very useful when reinforcing your point. Repeat the key phrase you want your audience to remember, e.g. 'And again I say that we strongly oppose the proposition that we are closer to the US than the EU.'
- **Imperatives:** These are orders or statements used to tell the audience what to do. Use imperatives sparingly as too many orders make you sound like a bully, e.g. 'Stand up to the proposition. Reject their argument. Support the right of the individual against the might of the totalitarian state.'
- **Compliment/insult:** You can compliment your audience and subtly insult your opposition by using statements like, 'Such a learned audience can not help but support my team rather than follow the misguided ramblings of the opposition.' Remember to be subtle as heavy-handed insulting of the other team just results in you sounding like a bad loser.

4. Structure
Vary your sentence length and structure throughout your speech. Long-winded sentences just lose the attention of the audience. Short snappy sentences that are focused will keep your speech to the point. Interweave them with explanatory sentences and references to support the points you make. Above all else, your argument must follow a logical sequence, therefore it **must** be planned.

5. Anecdotes
Anecdotes are brief humorous stories that have a relevance to the speech you are making. They may be personal or possibly references to film or television, e.g. 'As Joey once said to Chandler in the comedy *Friends*, there are two important things in life, food and food. No where is this more true than in the third world where starvation is a fact of life.'

6. Quotation
You may quote from any source that supports your argument: poetry, song lyrics, politicians, films, etc. Make sure that you credit the appropriate person in your speech, e.g. 'As Martin Luther King once said "I have a dream" and today I also have a dream.'

SAMPLE QUESTIONS

1. The motion for your next debate is: 'The Irish are the litter louts of Europe.' Write the speech you would write for or against the motion. (*Junior Certficate, 2001*)
2. Write out the speech you would make for or against the motion 'That the youth of today are cruel and unfeeling.' (*Junior Certficate, 2000*)
3. Write out the speech you would make for or against the motion 'That life was never better for young people than it is today.'
4. The motion for your next debate is: 'That bloodshed has never achieved anything.' Write out the speech you would make for or against the motion. (*Junior Certficate, 1998*)

Dialogue

You may be asked to write your essay in dialogue format. This format allows you to write your story as a script. There are certain guidelines you should follow for this style of writing.

- You may include stage directions and instructions for the characters throughout the piece.
- Follow the punctuation guidelines below.
- Include instructions as to tone of voice etc. in brackets after the character's name.
- Allow yourself space to lay out the dialogue clearly.
- Keep the dialogue realistic but also interesting. You still aim to capture the reader's attention.
- Plan your script. Don't allow it to wander aimlessly.

Use your study of Drama for Paper 2 for inspiration and guidelines on how to improve your dialogues. The following guidelines may prove useful.

Punctuation for dialogue

Background:
Detail any information you wish to include at the beginning of the extract, e.g. setting, positions of the characters on stage, relationships between the characters.

Harry: Hi Jane

Jane: Hi Harry! (Turning towards him)

Harry: (Anxiously twisting his cap in his hands) Eh . . . I was wondering if I could ask you a question?

| Characters' names followed by colon. | What the characters say. There is no need for inverted commas. |

Read the following example of how a dialogue is written.

Our Day Out

Keeper: Are you supposed to be in charge of this lot?

Mrs Kay: Why, what's the matter?

Keeper: Children? They're not bloody children, they're animals. It's not the zoo back there, this is the bloody zoo, here.

Briggs: Excuse me! Would you mind controlling your language and telling me what's going on?

Keeper (*ignores him, pushes past and confronts the* kids): Right, where are they? *Innocent faces and replies of 'What?', 'Where's what?'*

Keeper: You know bloody well what . . .

Briggs (*intercepting him*): Now look, this has just gone far enough. Would you . . .
          He is interrupted by the loud clucking of a hen.
          The keeper *strides up to a* kid *and pulls open his jacket. A bantam hen is revealed.*

Keeper   (*taking the hen, addresses the other* kids): Right, now I want the rest.
          There is a moment's hesitation before the floodgates are opened. Animals appear from every conceivable hiding-place.
          Briggs glares as the animals are rounded up.
          The kids *stay in place, waiting for the thunder.*

Briggs: I trusted you lot. And this is the way you repay me. (*Pause as he fights to control his anger.*) I trusted all of you but it's obvious that trust is something you know nothing about.

Ronson: Sir we only borrowed them.

Briggs (*screaming*): Shut up lad! Is it any wonder that people won't do anything for you? The moment we start to treat you like real people, what happens? Well that man was right. You act like animals, animals.

Mrs Kay: Come on now, take the animals back.
          The kids *relieved at finding a way to go. As they move off* Briggs *remains.*

Briggs: And that's why you're treated like animals, why you'll always be treated like animals.

Kids (*sing very quietly as they exit*):
>   Our day out
>   Our day out

Briggs (*alone on stage*): Animals!
>   *Blackout.*

From *Our Day Out* by Willie Russell

QUESTIONS

1. You arrive home from a party at 3 a.m. having promised your parents you would be in by 11.30 p.m. You overhear your parents' conversation. Write out in dialogue form what you have heard. You may give the conversation a relevant setting and, if you wish, intersperse the dialogue with unspoken observations of your own on what is said. (*Junior Certificate, 2000*)

2. Write out the conversation (in dialogue form) that might occur between a parent and teenager after the parent comes home from a parent/teacher meeting. (*Junior Certificate, 1997*)

3. You have been caught by your father or mother doing something foolish or something that is considered wrong. Write out the dialogue that then takes place. You may set the scene with a short piece of narrative writing if you wish. (*Junior Certificate, 1996*)

4. Imagine you have overheard a conversation between your mother and an aunt or grandmother about what is to become of you. Write out in dialogue form what you heard. You may give the conversation a relevant setting and, if you wish, intersperse the dialogue with unspoken observations of your own on what is said. (*Junior Certificate, 1995*)

5. Compose the conversation that you imagine might have occurred between the two men in the picture below. (*Junior Certificate, 2001*)

Discursive Essay

A discursive essay is your opportunity to discuss a topic and construct an argument around it using examples and supporting your point of view.

- Your discussion should be logical and follow a sequence of thought.
- You should engage the reader from the start.
- Use statements and references (as with the debate speech) to support your points.
- As the discursive essay is your personal thoughts on a topic you should use personal anecdotes and insights to enlighten the reader as to why you hold a particular point of view.

Read the following discursive essay.

Heaven Preserve the Family from Teenage Girls

Teenagers, of each generation, are an extremely interesting lot. The reason for this is that there has never been a precedent for those of any particular period.

I am at present the keeper of one full fledged teenager, a late twentieth-century model, who celebrates her fourteenth birthday this month. In September I shall add a male teenager to my collection. He is only twelve but already showing many symptoms.

The modern female teenager is a vegetarian. This diet does not actually encompass the consumption of many vegetables, merely the refusal to eat meat. Neither, in any conventional sense, are meals taken. Feeding behaviour is instead akin to that of a ruminant, with more or less continual grazing on sweets, Coca-Cola and chips, with an occasional McDonald's filet-o-fish.

She is extremely clean. Baths and showers are taken at least twice daily. *These are not quick dunk-and-scrub affairs, but prolonged aquatic manoeuvres, involving the employment of vast quantities of hot water spiced with overpriced unguents, lotions and potions*. It does not matter how many of these are held in stock in the bathroom – more are always required.

Despite this obsession with bodily hygiene, her bedroom is a nesting ground for vermin of all types, as clothes, shoes, sheet music, incomplete homework, empty bottles of Body Shop preparations and copies of *Just Seventeen* magazine are piled into the tumuli on the floor.

Susceptibility to squalor is perhaps not unique to this generation of adolescents: what is novel is the sheer quantity of material possessions with which they are capable of demonstrating their indifference to conventional standards of domestic order.

Notwithstanding her technical facility with satellite receiver, video recorder and computer equipment of all types, she has yet to work out the basic operation of the washing machine or vacuum cleaner.

She has achieved a sophisticated understanding of finance, knowing that money does not grow on trees, but comes through a hole in the wall, accessed by means of her father's cash card. Although she has hundreds and hundreds of pounds a year passing through her bank account, receiving a lavish monthly allowance, with cash top-ups from grandparents at birthdays and Christmas, she expects that all significant costs will be met by her parents.

She is fit for postgraduate employment in the civil service, having maintained an obsessional secrecy over all information concerning her social life.

She is embarrassed to be seen in public with her parents, who are, variously, 'sad' and 'tragic'. Although not so sad and tragic as to be above delivering, on her seventeenth birthday, a white Volkswagen Beetle (she hopes).

Despite the vast sums that are expended and the bulging closet of garments available, her clothing is always inappropriate to the season; she will happily go out in the middle of winter wearing only a T-shirt.

When she is not being completely charming – a transient condition invariably related to her need to be driven to a distant shopping precinct to resupply herself with unguents or compact discs – she employs to her parents and sibling a manner of address interspersed with frequent contemptuous groans and grunts. These sound effects are triggered whenever a suggestion is made that she might tidy her bedroom, or take upon herself the exhausting imposition of transporting an empty crisp packet to a bin.

You might ask why I continue to finance this creature, and the answer, of course, is that in approximately ten or fifteen years, she will, I trust, provide me with the material to write a column on the joys of twenty-first-century grandparenting, allowing me in my dotage to coo at children who go home after tea.

'Heaven Preserve the Family from Teenage Girls' by Jonathan Miller
(Junior Certificate, 1998)

QUESTIONS

1. What anecdotal evidence does the writer use to support his argument?
2. What type of person is his daughter? What evidence is there in the extract to support this point of view?
3. The writer uses a variety of descriptive techniques to describe the aftermath of his daughter. Identify some of the techniques used.
4. The writer uses hyperbole (exaggeration) to make his point. Give some examples.

On the same topic of 'teenagers', the following piece looks at the issue from a different perspective. Read the extract and answer the questions that follow.

We Are Not a Sub-species

The worst thing about being a teenager is the word 'teenager'. Being a teenager doesn't feel any different from being a normal person. I don't seem to be undergoing any emotional traumas, or identity crises – I must be letting somebody down. The word teenager prevents some people from treating adolescents as young adults; in their eyes we become a kind of sub-species.

My sixth form used to be regularly visited by various speakers. One week the local insurance man came. In an unfortunate effort to obtain group participation and yet remain in control of talk, he treated 200 intelligent 18-year-olds like a load of morons. Smiling benignly, he said: 'Now what do we find under roads?' The answers he received – worms, moles, and dead insurance men – were not what he was looking for. Actually it was pipelines. Ask a stupid question! The point is, that man would not have spoken to adults in the same way, so why to teenagers? If you treat people like idiots, they act like idiots.

There might not be that much difference between a 34-year-old and a 38-year-old, but there's a hell of a lot of difference between a 14-year-old and an 18-year-old. When I was 13, I though post-primary school was the ultimate in maturity. Now at the worldly age of 18, 16 seems a mere nothing.

The word teenager is misleading because it leads to generalisations and it is so derogatory. For many adults there is no such thing as a teenager who doesn't like discos – if you happen not to, as many teenagers don't – they label you as an awkward, anti-social adolescent.

For a short time I was a waitress in a diners' club. The average age of the staff was 19, that of the clientele about 40. We, the staff, used to watch amused and slightly disgusted as overweight middle-aged swingers, who in the light of day would claim that discos were a load of teenage nonsense, jerked violently around to the latest hits – as they say. (They were either dancing or having heart attacks – I couldn't quite tell.) If, in the eyes of adults, 'teenage culture' is such a contemptible thing, why, given the opportunity, do they throw themselves into it with so much enthusiasm and a lot less style?

I may be cynical, but I think it is partly due to jealousy. Some adults patronise teenagers because they are envious of their youth and because the respect they don't get from their peers they demand from their juniors. Even on the lofty level of our local tennis club, this type of jealousy rears its head, or rather, swings its racket. If we were to put forward our strongest women's team, it would consist entirely of teenage girls. Of course, this never happens. The elder women play by virtue of their age, not skill. After all, teenage girls don't count as women.

If there is such as thing as a teenager, it refers to a state of mind and not a particular age range. At 20, you don't automatically become an adult because you've dropped the 'teen' in your age. Unfortunately, 'teenager' has come to connote things like selfishness, irresponsibility, and arrogance. This means there are a lot of adults around who are still teenage. Equally, if maturity is measured in attributes, such as compassion and tolerance, and not merely the number of years you've totted up, then there are a lot of adult teenagers around.

I would like the word 'teenager' to be banned, but I suppose that will never happen, as a lot of people would stop making a lot of money.

'We Are Not a Sub-species' (edited) by Lois McNay
(Junior Certificate, 1995)

QUESTIONS

1. How does the writer feel about the word 'teenager'?
2. How does the writer support her argument? Give examples.
3. What is the writer's opinion of adults?
4. Identify some of the writing techniques used by the writer to put forward her argument. Give examples.

EXAM QUESTIONS

Write a discursive essay on one of the following topics.
1. What the clothes you wear say about you. *(Junior Certificate, 2002)*
2. Life's little luxuries. *(Junior Certificate, 2002)*
3. People that make the world a better place. *(Junior Certificate, 2001)*
4. Looking forward to things is always better than the reality. What do you think? *(Junior Certificate, 2000)*
5. The thing about myself I would most like to change. *(Junior Certificate, 1999)*
6. The generation gap. *(Junior Certificate, 1998)*
7. Heroes *(Junior Certificate, 1998)*

Diary Entry and Letter

The main difference between a diary entry and the other types of essay is that it must be written in the first person, i.e. 'I'. It is a personal account of events and is therefore by its nature biased and subjective. When writing a diary entry or a letter it is worthwhile noting the following points:

- You must write in the first person, 'I', throughout.
- You should include personal observations, hopes and fears.
- You must write in the past tense as a diary is usually a reflective piece written at the end of the day reflecting on the events of the day.
- You can mention hopes for the future.
- Letters are similar to diary entries as they are first person accounts written to another party, giving them insights into events from your perspective.

Read the letter below and answer the questions that follow.

Letter to Daniel (adapted)

Daniel Patrick Keane was born on 4 February 1996.

Hong Kong, February 1996

My dear son, it is six o'clock in the morning on the island of Hong Kong. You are asleep cradled in my left arm and I am learning the art of one-handed typing. Your mother, more tired yet more happy than I've ever known her, is sound asleep in the room next door and there is a soft quiet in the apartment.

Since you've arrived, days have melted into night and back again and we are learning a new grammar, a long sentence whose punctuation marks are feeding and winding and nappy changing and these occasional moments of quiet.

Your coming has turned me upside down and inside out. So much that seemed essential to me has, in the past few days, taken on a different colour. Like many foreign correspondents I know, I have a lived a life, that on occasion, has veered close to the edge: war zones, natural disasters, darkness in all its shapes and forms.

In a world of insecurity and ambition and ego, it's easy to be drawn in, to take chances with our lives, to believe that what we do and what people say about us is reason enough to gamble with death. Now, looking at your sleeping face, inches from me, listening to your occasional sigh and gurgle, I wonder how I could have ever thought glory and prizes and praise were sweeter than life.

And it's also true that I am pained, perhaps haunted is a better word, by the memory, suddenly so vivid now, of each suffering child I have come across on my journeys. To tell you the truth, it's nearly too much to bear at this moment to even think of children being hurt and abused and killed. And yet looking at you, the images come flooding back. Ten-year-old Andi Mikail dying from napalm burns on a hillside in Eritrea, how his voice cried out, growing ever more faint when the wind blew dust on to his wounds. Last October, in Afghanistan, when you were growing inside your mother, I met Sharja, aged twelve. Motherless, fatherless, guiding me through the grey ruins of her home, everything was gone, she told me. And I knew that, for all her tender years, she had learned more about loss than I would likely understand in a lifetime. Daniel, these memories explain some of the fierce protectiveness I feel for you, the tenderness and the occasional moments of blind terror when I imagine anything happening to you.

But there is something more, a story from long ago that I will tell you face to face, father to son, when you are older. It's a very personal story but it's part of the picture. It begins thirty-five years ago in a big city on a January morning with snow on the ground and a woman walking to hospital to have her first baby. She's walking because there is no money and everything of value has been pawned to pay for the alcohol to which her husband has become addicted.

On the way, a taxi driver notices her sitting, exhausted and cold, in the doorway of a shop and he takes her to hospital for free. Later that day, she gives birth to a baby boy and, just as you are to me, he is the best thing she has ever seen. Her husband comes that night and weeps with joy when he sees his son. He is truly happy. Hungover, broke, but in his own way happy, for they were both young and in love with each other and their son.

But Daniel, time had some bad surprises in store for them. The cancer of alcoholism ate away at the man and he lost his family. This was not something he meant to do or wanted to do. It just was.

Yet now, Daniel, I must tell you that when you let out your first powerful cry in the delivery room of the Adventist Hospital and I became a father, I thought of your grandfather and, foolish though it may seem, hoped that in some way he could hear, across the infinity between the living and the dead, your proud statement of arrival. For if he could hear, he would recognise the distinct voice of family, the sound of hope and new beginnings that you and all your innocence and freshness have brought to the world.

(Junior Certificate, 1997)

QUESTIONS

1. How does the writer set the scene for the reader?
2. What does he want to tell his child about events in the past?
3. What are his hopes for the future?
4. How has the birth of his son affected him?

Read the following extract from the novel *Death and Nightingales* by Eugene McCabe.

Death and Nightingales

Clonoula,
9 August 1881

My Dear Elizabeth,

Now I begin to see the place you describe. Naples is a long way from home.

You ask me for news. It's quiet here mostly. Yesterday I rowed out to Corvey, your island. The business of punting cattle out and back to thirty unmannered acres is a doubtful one. Today I posted to Enniskillen for Matthew Gemmel's funeral. He cut his throat poor fellow. Loneliness, the minister said. Again there are rumours afloat that I am to sell Clonoula, that the quarry is bankrupt and that I have become an inveterate night tippler. All wishful talk from my well-wishers hereabouts!

Our meadows are all scythed, saved and stacked in the barns, lofts and haggard; about three hundred rucks in all. The yard smells sweet and summery. Our cattle will be content this winter.

Soon I'll have hooks out to the barley and pullers out to the flax. Did I tell you I tried out a field of linseed? It flowers blue like the grotto at Capri you wrote me about. People stare at it. It's worth coming back to Fermanagh to view such a wonder: a blue field under a black sky.

Let me say now that I would love to see you home again. I can give you a few good reasons for returning. Firstly you belong here, you play the piano well and sing sweetly when persuaded! For the six months you were here, you managed the yard and dairy better than any working steward. Every room in the house is missing your presence! Will you think about this? I promise to conduct myself as honourably as any man in Ulster. Do you believe me? Do I believe myself? Absolutely.

The new dispensary doctor is a young man called Bell. I called on him after Gemmel's funeral. He tells me my chest pains are 'intercostal neuritis' and that I'm as healthy as a goat. I think you'd like him, a quirky sense of humour, a real Ulsterman.

I grow benign with the years believe me, and every day I miss you.

You have at all times my deepest love,

Papa

From *Death and Nightingales* by Eugene McCabe

Questions

Write an essay based on one of the following titles.

1. Imagine you are present at a great event in history. Write out in diary form your personal reactions to the event. (*Junior Certificate, 1999*)
2. Write a letter to some public figure or leader in any part of the world on the subject of peace. (*Junior Certificate, 1997*)
3. A teacher new to your school has just taught your class for the first time. Imagining you are that teacher, write a personal letter to a friend in which you bring out your thoughts and feelings, the atmosphere in the classroom, and how you felt when the class was over. In particular, try to convey a lively picture of the class in action. (*Junior Certificate, 1995*)

3
Functional Writing

The Functional Writing section of the exam is worth thirty marks. The aim of this section is to write *according to the task* required. The language used is mainly formal, so avoid the use of abbreviations or slang. Try to be as brief and as clear as you can while carrying out all that the task requires. There are no extra marks for filling up pages with irrelevant asides.

There is usually a choice of two or three tasks given to choose from.

The different types of questions asked are:

LETTERS

- Of reference
- For job application (with CV)
- To an author
- To a newspaper
- As an agony aunt
- Of complaint

SPEECHES

- On a topic
- Of welcome or of farewell
- Pep talks
- Proposal

REVIEWS

- Of a CD, film, play or novel

ARTICLE

- For a tourist brochure (persuasive)
- or a newspaper (factual)

REPORT

- On details given (e.g. survey)

FACTUAL DESCRIPTION

- Of a photograph
- Set of instructions

Letters

There are two types of letters:
- Formal/business letters
- Informal/personal letters.

In the Junior Certificate exam the formal letter is most frequently requested. However it would be wise to be familiar with both types of letters.

PERSONAL LETTER

Personal letters are letters of a personal nature, e.g. to a pen-pal. They are informal and therefore the language used can be conversational and friendly. It is important to be aware of layout and punctuation, as there are marks awarded for this.

Layout:

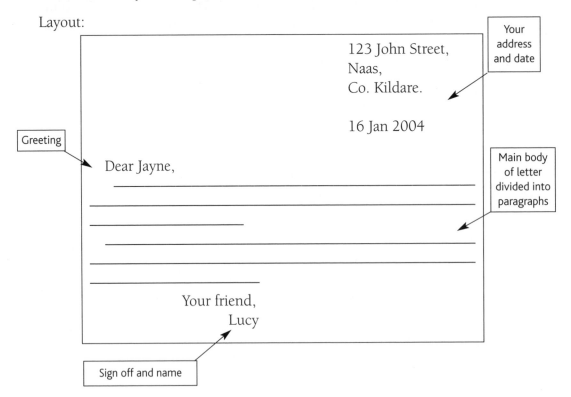

Address: Your address is written on the top right-hand corner of the page. It may be slanted or aligned, but above all it should be neat. Allow adequate room for the address. Each line begins with a capital letter and ends with a comma, except the last line, which ends with a full stop.

Date: The date can be written in various forms e.g. 16–01–04, or 16/01/04 or as above.

Greeting: In a personal letter the greeting should be informal and should only use the first name of the person you are writing to.

Sign off: Several versions are acceptable, e.g. your friend, all my love, see you soon etc. The first letter of the first word only should be a capital letter.

Make sure you answer the question asked. Don't go off on a tangent and miss the point. For this purpose a brief plan is useful.

SAMPLE QUESTION

Write a personal letter to a friend accepting or refusing an invitation to join them on a skiing holiday.

---

24 Sycamore Grove,
Newton,
Co. Cork.
24 Jan. '04

Dear Jane,

I am shocked, horrified and appalled to read the contents of your letter! How could you do this to me? After all we have been through! All those years planning the ideal break! And now you do this!

Of course I would love to join you and the gang for a week skiing in February. Of course I would be delighted to travel to Andorra, learn to ski with the professionals and relax with the nightly après ski entertainments, but have you forgotten something? I am sitting my Junior Cert. exams this year. My mocks begin on the 24 February — the very day that you intend to travel! My parents would never allow me to miss school at this crucial stage. Oh cruel, cruel fate!

I must remain here, chained to my books, studying into the wee hours of the morning, while you go on the trip of a lifetime. Think of me while you are careering down the slopes with the wind in your ears — I will be at my desk with nothing but French verbs to keep me amused!

I remain your friend, despite this thoughtlessness, and wish you the best for your trip. Bring me back a small memento!

Yours inconsolably,

Cathy.

QUESTIONS

1. Write a letter to a friend describing your experience of a match or concert you attended.
2. Write a letter to a pen-pal explaining why you can't visit them as planned this summer.
3. You are away from home on a school exchange. Write a letter home to your parents asking for more spending money.
4. You are visiting your elderly aunt. Write a letter to a friend describing the atmosphere in the house, your activities and plans for your return home.
5. You are June, the 'agony aunt' for a teen magazine. Write a reply to the following letter from the magazine problem page. The reply should be approximately 200 words in length (about one page).

Dear June,

I am writing to you for help because I am so terribly unhappy. Everything was fine until last year, when my family moved here from another part of the country. I left all my friends behind and had to start at a new school. I was quite popular in my old school and had lots of friends, but since starting in my new school I seem to have made no friends at all.

My family don't understand why I am so miserable and keep encouraging me to go out with my 'new friends'. Nobody seems to like me. What can I do?

                                                                                  A Very Unhappy Reader.

(Junior Certificate, 2000)

FORMAL LETTER

Formal letters are used in business or while conducting matters of a formal nature with people you don't know personally. The types of letters vary from letters of complaint to job applications, but the format remains the same. While this format is quite similar to the personal letter, the addition of the address of the recipient is important. The language used in this type of letter is more formal and serious than the personal letter. Don't use slang. The full name of the person you are writing to should be included where possible. Never use the first name only as this is too informal.

Layout:

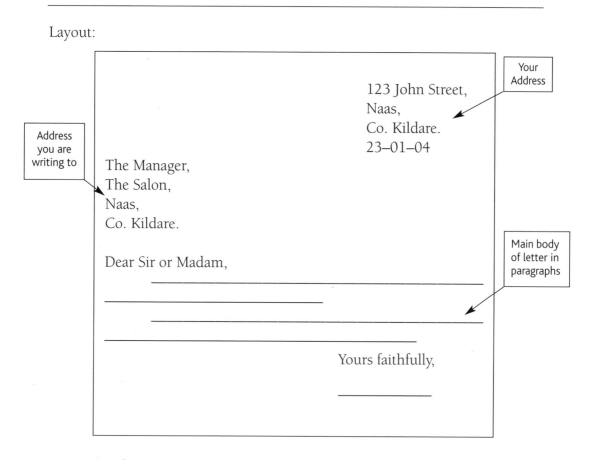

Greeting: If you know the name of the person you are writing to, your letter should address them personally, e.g. Dear Mr. Jones. If not, you address your letter to 'Dear Sir or Madam', or 'To whom it may concern'.

Main body of letter: The formal letter needs to be well structured and should be planned. Usually two or three paragraphs are sufficient. Don't ramble, you must stick to the point.

Closing: If you don't know the name of the person you are writing to you end with 'Yours faithfully'. If you do know their name you end the letter with 'Yours sincerely'.

SAMPLE ANSWER

Q. Write a letter of application in response to the following advertisement.

Trainee Mechanic required. No experience necessary. Apply in writing to Nolan's Garage, Main St., Tullow, Co. Carlow.

Sunday Independent, 18 January 2004

Plan

Paragraph 1: Where you saw the advertisement, position advertised.

Paragraph 2: Your age, qualifications, experience.

Paragraph 3: Your hobbies/interests.

Paragraph 4: Enclosed CV, available for interview.

---

168 The Crescent,
Tullow,
Co. Carlow.
19–01–04

The Manager,
Nolan's Garage,
Main Street,
Tullow,
Co. Carlow.

Dear Sir or Madam,

I am writing to apply for the position of Trainee Mechanic as advertised in the Sunday Independent of 18 January.

At present I am a third year student at Colomba's Secondary School and I am currently studying for my Junior Certificate exams. I have worked as a pump attendant for the past two months in Lawler's Garage in Carlow town.

I am interested in pursuing a career as a car mechanic and I regularly service and maintain my mother's car. I am hard working and eager to learn.

I enclose a curriculum vitae and the names of two referees. I am available for interview at any time. I will able to start work as soon as I finish my exams. I look forward to hearing from you soon.

Yours faithfully,
Andrew Butler

Formal Letters should always contain an element of formal style.

- The language used should be clear and to the point.
- Avoid excessive descriptions.
- Stick to the point.
- Keep the tone factual.

QUESTIONS

1. Write a letter to the author of any text you have studied, telling him/her whether or not you enjoyed it, and explaining why. *(Junior Certificate, 2002)*

2. You need a reference letter from your principal to secure a summer job. Write the letter you would like him/her to supply you with. The address you use should not be that of your actual school, nor should you use your own name. *(Junior Certificate, 2001)*

   (N.B. Read this question carefully! Write the reference not a letter to the principal asking for a reference.)

3. A letter has appeared in a daily newspaper claiming that 'teenagers nowadays have no moral standards'. Write a letter of reply in which you respond to this charge. *(Junior Certificate, 1999)*

4. You are applying for the position of bank manager of your school bank. Make out the brief CV you would submit and write the accompanying letter of application for the job. *(Junior Certificate, 1999)*

5. When you return to school next September you will be going into the Transition Year. Shortly after the start of the school year, as part of the Transition Year programme, you will be going out on work experience for two weeks. You are expected, in advance, to find a suitable workplace. Write out the **letter** you would send to an employer telling him/her what the Transition Year is, requesting work experience, explaining why you would like that kind of work and saying what you hope to gain from the experience. The main purpose of the letter is to persuade the employer to take you on for the two weeks. *(Junior Certificate, 1996)*

Hints

Question 5 above has already planned your letter for you:

Paragraph 1: Explain what the Transition Year is

Paragraph 2: Request work experience

Paragraph 3: Explain why you would like it and what you hope to gain

Paragraph 4: Conclusion

The examiner has also pointed out the writing style needed i.e. persuasive. Make sure you sound positive and persuasive throughout the letter. Enthusiasm is your greatest asset!

Question 4 above also asks for a 'brief CV'. Use the following CV as a guideline. Keep the same headings and fill in your own details as relevant.

CURRICULUM VITAE

Personal details

Name: Mary Murphy
Address: 16 Grange Heights, Cavan.
Telephone: 0404–262121
Mobile: 087–1231234
Date of Birth: 26–2–1990

Education

2001–To date   St Mary's Secondary School, Cavan.
1995–2001   St Killian's Primary School, Cavan.

Examinations Taken

2004 Junior Certificate Examination

Subject	Level	Grade
English	H	B
Irish	H	C
Maths	O	B
History	H	A
Geography	H	C
Science	O	D
Business Studies	O	B
French	H	C
Art	H	B
CSPE	–	B

Work Experience

Date	Employer	Position Held
May–Aug 2004	Kenny's Shop	Shop Assistant
June–Aug 2003	Summer Camp	Art Leader

Hobbies/Interests

I have an active interest in art especially watercolours. I have helped in local summer art courses for children. I also enjoy cinema, reading and theatre. I am the captain of my local camogie team.

Referees

Mr S. Dunleavy   Mr P. Kenny
Principal   Owner/Manager
St Mary's Secondary   Kenny's Shop
Cavan   Cavan

Signed: _____

Date: _____

Speeches

While writing a speech you must always be aware of the audience that you are addressing. You must aim to capture their attention and keep it. There are a number of ways to do this, which vary according to the type of speech you are writing.

You must first ask yourself what is the aim of the speech, as this will dictate the tone used. In recent exam papers the three main types of speeches asked for were:

- **A pep talk to a team**: This will be full of enthusiasm and helpful advice, occasionally berating members of the team who are not pulling their weight. But the overall aim is to be inspirational and encouraging!

  Use your own experience of being a member of a school or club team to write the pep talk. Avoid using bad language. While you may argue that it adds authenticity, it does give a bad impression of your writing skills. See if you can inspire fear and dedication without resorting to bad language; it will expand your writing skills!

- **A welcoming speech/farewell speech**: This speech will be more formal than the preceding one. You are representative of your peers and are welcoming or saying goodbye on their behalf.

  Plan this speech carefully. Give yourself something to say. A welcoming speech and one of farewell may include details of past achievements as well as future plans. Use humour where appropriate but don't be insulting.

- **A debate speech/speech on a topic**: The aim of this speech is to persuade the audience of the validity of your argument. You should be persuasive, informative and entertaining, but above all stick to the topic in question.

  Look back on the ingredients of a good speech in the last section. Elements of writing style such as the opening statement and use of factual reference remain the same. Remember you are trying to persuade your audience of the validity of your argument, so make sure your argument is well supported and use references and humour as well as elements of rhetoric to win them over.

QUESTIONS

1. You are the captain of a team playing in the final of a major competition. Your team is losing at half-time. Write out the pep talk you would give to the team. (*Junior Certificate, 2002*)
2. The principal of your school is leaving. You have been nominated by the Junior Certificate pupils in your school to prepare a speech for the occasion.

Write out the speech you would make to a gathering of staff and pupils on the principal's final day in the school. (*Junior Certificate, 2000*)

3. You have been asked to nominate a pupil in your class for the 'Student of the Year' award. Write in a persuasive style the nomination speech you would make in favour of this individual. (*Junior Certificate, 1999*)

4. You have been asked to give a five minute talk on why we should do Media Studies in school. Write out the talk you would give. (*Junior Certificate, 1998*)

5. You wish to start a club or society in your school. Its aim can be the promotion of debating a particular sport, a hobby, or any activity or combination of activities in which you are interested. Write out the speech you would make to your schoolmates outlining your ideas for the club or society and your motives for founding it, explaining how it might operate, and encouraging your audience to join. (*Junior Certificate, 1996*)

Reviews

A review is usually a personal opinion of a play, film, CD or book. When writing a review you should include the following:

- Full title, including author, director, band or performer.
- Brief background information.
- Summary of play, album or book etc. without giving away the ending or significant details.
- Your opinion: the high points (e.g. the actors, the script, the lyrics, the special effects) and the low points or weaknesses.

If you liked it you should be enthusiastic and encourage others to see or hear it. If you hated it you might offer some constructive criticism and possibly see some good points.

An example of a review

A BOY'S OWN BOOK

We all know children can be messy. Especially on the beach. But this is more than messy – it's scary. And deeply disturbing.

A group of English schoolboys have just survived a plane crash and end up on a deserted paradise island.

At first all seems hunky dory, but eventually 'the beast' rears his ugly head and the boys' initial attempt at setting up a civilised government collapses into tribal fury and demonic anarchy. Paradise island becomes an infernal territory where the Lord of the Flies and other satanic beings hold sway.

$\longrightarrow$

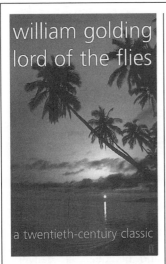

william golding
lord of the flies

a twentieth-century classic

It's exactly 50 years since William Golding's troubling novel was published, and it is a measure of the haunting potency and limpid prose of this book, not to mention the narrative skill and philosophical lucidity of its author, that once you read it you cannot conceive of a world when it did not exist.

Male Lit Crit students may have resented having to plough through Nelly Deane's monologues in *Wuthering Heights*, or the rather colourless prose of *Silas Marner*, but no male with an average deposit of testosterone or a decent dollop of humanity could fail to be wowed and all shook up by *Lord of the Flies*.

The 225-page novel is partly a straightforward, nasty account of what happens when a group of young men discover the bestial in themselves; partly a phantasmagoric parable about the ineradicable tendency of humans to practise inhumanity to fellow men; partly a chilling parody of classic island novels like Ballantyne's *Coral Island* or Stevenson's *Treasure Island*.

William Golding's view of humanity, of even young humanity, may seem depressingly cynical to some, but in fact it's just standard Christian teachings – post-Fall man is fallen man and thus doomed to create his own hell.

But bleak as that all sounds, *Lord of the Flies* is not a bleak read. In fact it is a richly satisfying, atmospheric, hypnotic book full of vividly drawn characters and deftly sketched locations.

Golding, who died in 1993, wrote several other novels (*The Spire*, *Pincher Martin*), but probably won the Nobel Prize for Literature (in 1983) for this book alone.

Declan McCormack,
Sunday Independent,
4 April 2004

QUESTIONS

1. Write a review for your local newspaper of your favourite CD or tape. (*Junior Certificate, 2001*)
2. Write for your school magazine a review of any one of the following:
- A film or video which you have recently seen
- A favourite tape or CD
- A play or show attended by you.

Give the name of the film, video, tape, CD, play or show that you are reviewing. (*Junior Certificate, 1995*)

SAMPLE ANSWER

PIRATES OF THE CARIBBEAN: THE CURSE OF THE BLACK PEARL

(Walt Disney Pictures/Jerry Bruckheimer Production)
Director: Gore Verbinski
137 mins

This swashbuckling adventure tells the story of the roguish Captain Jack Sparrow (Johnny Depp) and his entanglements with his former crewmates of the *Black Pearl* led by the nasty Captain Barbossa (Geoffrey Rush). Caught up in their disagreements are the beautiful Elizabeth (Keira Knightley) and her childhood friend Will Turner (Orlando Bloom). The *Black Pearl* is cursed, as are all the crewmates on board, but the release from the curse is somehow connected with a mysterious amulet worn by Elizabeth. Elizabeth is kidnapped by Barbossa and the gallant Will Turner needs to use all the methods at his disposal to rescue her, including befriending the dubious Captain Jack.

The attention to detail throughout the film is astounding, from the costumes and elaborate hairstyles to the replica pirate ships used in filming. Keira Knightley plays the typical damsel in distress but with slightly more gumption than most. Geoffrey Rush is excellent as the evil Captain Barbossa. His sneering persona dominates most scenes he is in. But without doubt the pearl of this film is the performance of Johnny Depp as Jack Sparrow. His depiction, based on a mixture of aging rock stars and the stereotypical pirate rogue, is comic and compelling. He gives new twists to an otherwise bland script and his deadpan delivery provides perfect comic timing.

Despite coming from Disney this film manages to give some spine-chilling scenes, helped significantly by the excellent special effects. Overall, well worth the price of admission. Good old fashioned story, well-drawn characters, a villainous villain, special effects that don't swamp the film itself and moments of real comedy. What more could you want from a film?

Article

There were two types of article asked for in recent exam papers:

- For a tourist brochure (persuasive)
- For a newspaper (factual/informative)

PERSUASIVE

In a persuasive article you are trying to persuade the reader to buy or avail of the goods or services on offer. The type of language used is exaggerated and enthusiastic. Typical of tourist brochures or estate agent blurbs, the language used is flowery and uses vivid imagery to persuade the reader to buy.

Phrases such as 'a peaceful haven', 'generously proportioned', 'superbly maintained' and 'a delightful aspect' are scattered throughout the piece. There is excessive use of adjectives such as: superb, charming, spacious, attractive, ample, exclusive and tranquil, and verbs such as nestled, tucked and bustling. Awareness of the audience is essential. In an 18–30 holiday brochure a nightspot might be described as 'a lively and a cosmopolitan mix', whereas a guidebook for the retired might refer to the same place as 'a bustling village with an ethnic feel'. Also the tone is overwhelmingly positive. A house that is a complete ruin is described as 'in need of refurbishment'.

A HEALTHY LIFE BY THE SEA GOOD FOR BODY AND SOUL

Sinead Deignan

THERE comes a point in every young adult's life where getting out of the rent circuit or your parents' gaff is an inevitable part of safeguarding your economic security, if not your sanity.

If you have €3,000 sitting in the bank and you are wondering what to do with it, cast your eye to the scenic sight of Portmarnock village and consider putting a booking deposit on one of the 40 apartments being released in Seabrook Manor.

Portmarnock is all about the great outdoors. It has the best of amenities for sailing, surfing and swimming.

The village is inundated with tennis, football and rugby clubs. There is also a very active cycling club that avails of the open scenery and quieter country roads.

Within close proximity to Seabrook Manor there is a horse riding club and an abundance of leisure and sporting facilities.

Where? Seabrook Manor, Portmarnock, Co Dublin
How Much? From €300,000
Who? Hooke & MacDonald and O'Farrell Cleere
How? Viewing today between 2.30 and 4.30
Why buy? Spacious and affordable homes by the sea

Some of the best golf courses in the country are only minutes away at Portmarnock Links, Portmarnock Golf Club and Malahide Golf Club.

With mile upon mile of sandy beaches only a short stroll from the development, the less active can take leisurely strolls breathing sea air that guarantees a solid night's sleep.

Of the 234 apartments in the Seabrook Manor development, 95 have already been sold. It is no wonder given the superb location.

→

Far enough away from the city to enjoy country life, the infrastructure provides a great network to and from Dublin proper.

Located opposite the Dart station, it is convenient to Howth, Sutton, Malahide with the added benefit of an excellent road network, readily accessible to the whole of Dublin and surrounding counties.

It is also on the bus route to and from the city.

Every conceivable amenity is close at hand, including fine shops, boutiques, restaurants, hotels and hostelries – all are within easy reach.

Designed by Fenton Simons Architects, these apartments are well-finished homes, conscious of light and space.

Covered by the Home Bond 10-Year Guarantee Scheme, they are exempt from stamp duty for owner occupiers.

INFORMATIVE

In a newspaper article the type of language used is usually factual. The aim is to present the reader with a detailed account of an event with relevant background information and an overview of events. The article is very structured.

- In the first paragraph the details of the event are outlined: time, date and people involved.
- The second paragraph develops the story by giving background information or a descriptive account of the event.
- The third paragraph will usually deal with the long-term effects of the event, or future plans or an overview of the problem/event.

HERO'S WELCOME FOR HOMEGROWN OLYMPIC WINNER

Melanie Finn

The tiny village of Johnstown came to a standstill yesterday as locals welcomed back their home-grown Olympic hero.

A carnival atmosphere prevailed in the Kildare town as Cian O'Connor arrived home to a red-carpet reception.

Hundreds poured into the town to make sure their party, one of several thrown for the gold medallist, was really one to remember.

Outside his mum Louise's house on the main street, where he lived until he was 19, a poster read 'Welcome home golden boy', along with photos of him in the front window.

Huge cheers erupted as the Kildare man rolled into town at 7.30 p.m. having swapped his winning horse Waterford Crystal for an open-topped Rolls-Royce.

Accompanied by his girlfriend Rachel Wyse and sister Philippa, his car was quickly surrounded by well wishers and children.

As he took out his medal and showed it to the crowd, Tina Turner's 'Simply the Best' blasted from the loudspeakers set up by local station KFM.

In a live broadcast, his grandfather Karl Mullen, who captained Ireland to triple crown victory in the 40s, paid tribute to his famous grandson.

'He is a wonderful young man. He will always surmount every obstacle. I'm very proud of him,' he said.

Cian told the crowd that although it was five years since he lived there, it was great seeing all the same faces again.

'I've been to several receptions this week but this one definitely takes the biscuit. Some of the kind words of the people were very moving. There's a lot of special people here.'

Irish Independent, 3 September 2004

QUESTIONS

1. Look at the photographs below.
   They are to be used in a tourist brochure to promote a luxury hotel and its surroundings as a holiday destination. Now write in an appropriate style, the text of the **article** that will accompany these photographs in the brochure.

   (Junior Certificate, 1999)

A

B

C

D

2. Your local Tourist Office has asked you to write a brief article of not more than 300 words on your locality for a brochure, which will be available for tourists who come to your area. Write out the **article** that you would submit for publication. The purpose of the article should be to enthuse tourists about your area, to entice them to spend a holiday there, and to give them some information about the history and the amenities of the place. *(Junior Certificate, 1996)*

3. Imagine you are a newspaper reporter. Write for your newspaper a **report** suggested by the photograph. Your report should be no longer than one page of your answer book. *(Junior Certificate, 1997)*

Report

The other type of report requested in the exam is an official report on a topic based on findings. This type of report is not intended for a newspaper, but instead would be presented to a committee or group. There is a basic format that you can adhere to, or change, according to your requirements.

As this report is based on findings you must outline why the report was carried out, what methods of research were used, what the findings were and the conclusions reached. The structure is as follows:

1. Title

What the report is about e.g. a survey of traffic problems in your local area.

2. Terms

Who carried out the report? For whom? Why?

For example: 'the report carried out by class 3A as requested by the board of management in order to implement a new policy for the school.'

3. Research

What kind of research was carried out? Survey? Questionnaire? Who was asked?

4. Results

What were the results of the survey? List in a factual manner without opinion the results of the survey or questionnaire.

5. Conclusions

What conclusions can you draw from the results as listed above? Your opinion should be supported by the facts as listed above in section 4.

6. Recommendations

What recommendations would you make based on the conclusions you listed above? These should be feasible but can be divided into short term and long-term goals.

7. Sign and Date

Sign on behalf of the group you represent and date the report.

QUESTIONS

1. The Transition Year class in your school carried out a survey of how the students in third year spent an average of €10 pocket money per week. Based on the figures supplied below write a report on this survey for your school magazine. *(Junior Certificate, 2002)*

Pocket Money Survey	Males	Females
food/soft drinks	3.90	2.40
leisure goods and services	2.70	1.90
clothing	1.00	2.40
personal goods	1.40	2.30
transport	1.00	1.00

Factual Description

(A) PHOTOGRAPHS

- When asked to accurately describe a photograph you should use clear, precise language.
- Divide the photograph into sections and deal with each separately, e.g. background, foreground, mid-ground.
- State the obvious e.g. it is a black and white photograph of a landscape; it is a colour photograph of an urban scene.
- Describe the expression on the faces of the people in the photograph.
- Use adjectives to describe the atmosphere, objects, people e.g. she has a weather-beaten face; it is a bleak landscape; they are enthusiastic/apathetic etc.

QUESTIONS

Write accurate descriptions of the following photographs.

A

B

C

D

(B) INSTRUCTIONS

- When writing instructions you should be clear and precise.
- List all necessary steps and divide up your answer into point format or number each stage.
- Don't assume any previous knowledge but don't talk down to the reader either.
- Explain any technical terms used.
- You could divide up your answer into preparations, steps and aftercare. Or whatever headings suit your task.
- Include any equipment needed.
- You could also give helpful hints as to how to avoid typical pitfalls.

QUESTIONS

1. Choose one of your favourite team games or board games and, for the benefit of a person who does not know how to play it, explain the purpose and general rules of the game. Your account should attempt to combine brevity and clarity. Give the name of the game you are describing. (*Junior Certificate, 1995*)
2. Write the instructions for one of the following: painting a room, mending a puncture, cooking your favourite meal, planting a tree.

Interview

You may be asked to write out the text of an interview with a famous person for publication in a magazine.

- Set the scene. Provide some background information to give the reader a context. Explain some previous successes or failures of the interviewee.
- Structure your answer into questions and answers. The answers should be significantly longer than the questions asked. Long lists of 'No comment' reveal nothing about the personality of the interviewee.
- Ask questions that are of interest to the readers but without being rude to the interviewee.
- End your piece with an overview of your opinion of the interviewee.

TV TUBE HEART

*Anthony Murnane,
broadcaster and journalist*

**Which TV shows did you
watch as a kid?**
I remember watching John
Craven's *Newsround* every
evening around 5pm. Here
was this guy – albeit with a
stunning array of woolly
jumpers – who sat in front
of the newsdesk. Wow!
Mind you, I chose the
anarchy of *Tiswas* on
Saturdays – the phantom
flan flinger beat Noel
Edmonds hands down.

What do you watch now?
My working hours mean
I've missed many of the
must-see TV shows of
recent years. With two kids
under four, *Balamory* and
Bob the Builder are staples.
For a break from the news
it's got to be *Black Books*,
Scrubs and *Curb Your
Enthusiasm*.

**Did you have a TV pin-
up?**
I could say too many to
mention but the simple
answer is no.

**Which TV shows would
you send to your Room
101?**
Any of those make-over
programmes – be they
about houses, gardens or
humans. And what is that
David Dickinson bloke all
about?

**Who was the best-ever
TV detective?**
I can never commit to any
of those six-hour, three-
part detective series, but
for entertainment value –
Peter Sellers' Inspector
Clousseau.

**Coronation Street or
EastEnders?**
I miss most of them
because of work but *Corrie*
has to win out – I don't
know nuffink about
EastEnders.

**If you had a million euro
to develop a TV show
what would you do with
it?**
I would give it to Network
2 to see if it could give it's
excellent late night news
programme *News on 2* a

regular time-slot that's not
after 11pm.

**Best newscaster of all
time?**
Jon Snow of Channel 4 is
hard to beat for his
knowledge, reporting
abilities and presentation
style. In the 80s I was
impressed by the BBC's
Michael Buerk who broke
the Ethiopian famine story
and then moved into the
studio. Oh, and Sharon Ní
Bheoláin said she'd kill me
if she didn't get a mention.

**Your most embarrassing
moment on TV?**
It involved 15 seconds of
footage featuring a dancing
cow in Spain. I couldn't get
the image out of my head
and unfortunately I had to
read an introduction to
another report. I couldn't,
and laughed my way
through the entire lead-in
before the next piece of
tape was rolled.

Anthony Murnane is a
presenter and producer of
RTÉ *News On 2* (after 11pm)
RTÉ Guide

QUESTION

1. You have interviewed for your school magazine a poet or writer with whose work you are familiar. Write out the text of the interview as you would submit it for publication. *(Junior Certificate, 2000)*

Agenda and Minutes of a Meeting

In any business, organisation or group, there are meetings to discuss ideas and finalise plans. There are set ways of organising and recording any kind of meeting and these are the agenda and the minutes.

The agenda is the list of topics to be discussed during the course of the meeting. The chairperson will usually run the meeting, decide who will speak next, finalise decisions and move on to the next topic. A typical agenda will look like this:

AGENDA
Date:

1. Minutes of the last meeting
2. Matters arising
3. Officers' reports
4. Orders of business
5. AOB (any other business)

---

1. Minutes

The minutes are the notes taken during the meeting (usually by the secretary of the group). All important points discussed, any objections and final decisions taken are all noted in the minutes. These notes are then referred to at the start of the next meeting to ensure that all relevant points are followed up on.

2. Matters arising

If there is any issue referred to in the minutes that needs to be updated or commented upon this is the time to do it.

3. Officers' reports

Each group or organisation will have people in certain positions (Treasurer, PRO, etc.) responsible for the running of the organisation. This is where they report on their activities since the last meeting.

4. Orders of business

This is where the chairperson adds in the issues that he/she would like discussed.

5. AOB

(Any other business) This is when anyone present at the meeting can raise issues they would like discussed.

QUESTIONS

1. Write out the agenda you think would be typical of a residents' association meeting.
2. Write out the minutes of a fictional county council meeting discussing the proposed introduction of paid parking in your locality. Take note of those who support the proposal and those who object along with their stated reasons.

4
Media Studies

The Media Studies section of the course allows you to examine various aspects of the communications media. You should be aware of how the media works, the purpose and aim of various aspects of the media and the effect it has.

Media, by definition, is any method by which information is communicated e.g. via television, the internet, through film and by telephone. In this course we are dealing with the mass media i.e. the way information is conveyed to a large audience simultaneously. Examples of this type of media are: television, radio, newspapers, magazines and advertising. You are expected to know how these various aspects of the media work, what effect they have and the key words associated with each aspect.

Past exam questions have focused on the following areas:

- Advertising
- Cartoons (political, humorous, satirical)
- Magazines
- Newspapers
- Television
- Radio

Advertising

By far the most frequently asked questions on the exam paper involve advertising. Advertising can take many forms: billboards, TV adverts and adverts placed in newspapers and magazines. However several aspects of advertising remain the same regardless of what media is used. You should be able to identify these in any advertisement on the exam paper and they should form the basis of your answer.

Purpose: The main purpose of any advertisement is to persuade you to buy the product or service. Most advertisements try to persuade you to buy by associating the product with a lifestyle that is desirable and by targeting a specific audience.

Product: The object, brand or service being advertised.

Slogan: The catch-phrase used to promote the product.

Logo: Emblem or symbol associated with the brand name.

Copy: The written text on an advertisement used to persuade you to buy the product.

Visuals: The colours, pictures and designs in the advertisement used to grab your attention and produce positive associations with the product.

Target audience: The type of person the advertisement is aimed at; consider their age, gender and lifestyle. The target audience are the people the advertisers want to buy the product. So in an advertisement for nappies the target audience are not babies but the parents that will buy the product, hence the use of images of happy smiling babies linked with pseudo-scientific language.

Most questions will ask you to analyse the advertisement. The following checklist will help you to structure your answer.

CHECKLIST

Visuals
Look at the overall layout of the advertisement. What are the main colours used?

- Are they bright vibrant colours such as yellow, red or orange? These usually convey a sense of warmth, vibrancy and energy.
- Are they cool, sterile colours such as blue or green? These usually convey a sense of cleanliness and are associated with peacefulness and tranquillity. Look for example at the number of advertisements for cleaning products that use these colours.
- Various colours have different associations. Decide what interpretation is relevant to the ad you are analysing.

White:	Innocence, peaceful, purity, simplicity.
Black:	Darkness, despair, bleak, modern, sleek, powerful.
Green:	Clean, growth, springtime, regenerating.
Blue:	Peaceful, tranquil, sea-like, clean, refreshing.
Red:	Danger, passion, emotional, vibrant.
Yellow:	Warmth, sun-like, happy.
Silver:	Modern, scientific, sleek, advanced.

Look at the associations you make with certain colours and build your own vocabulary from there.

If there are people in the visual, look at what they are doing.

- Are they running, jumping or sitting?
- What does this tell you about the people? Are they athletic, energetic or fun-loving?
- What is this trying to associate with the product?
- What are they wearing? Are they identified as being from a certain class or social grouping because of these clothes? Perhaps a businessman or a housewife?
- Is there stereotyping evident? (Stereotyping is the use of a standardised idea of a type of person e.g. the male stressed businessman.) Does the advertisement try to challenge our stereotypes e.g. using a female doctor or a male nurse?
- Look at the expressions on their faces. What emotion is conveyed: happiness, discontent, contentment, bewilderment or satisfaction? Again, what is this trying to associate with the product?
- Are the people and the lifestyle in the visual similar to the target audience e.g. age, gender, lifestyle?

What **lifestyle** is the advertisement trying to associate with this product? Look at the setting and the props used in the scene.

- Is the product associated with a jet-setting lifestyle? A rural country retreat? A hectic city life?
- Are traditional family values emphasised?

Is the slogan dominating the visual?

- If so, look at the shape, size and colour of the lettering.
- Does the colour echo the other colours in the advertisement? Does it provide a contrast? Is it eye-catching?
- Is the font trying to say something about the product? Does it use *an old style of writing* to portray certain characteristics of the product, such as its tradition? Or does it use **a very modern script** to denote its modernity and technological advances?

Finally does the advertisement contain an endorsement by a celebrity? By associating a sporting figure or a celebrity with their product they can associate the celebrity's success with their product, e.g. the use of a sports drink or a certain type of football boot. They also associate the product with the lifestyle of the celebrity.

Copy

The copy is any written text on the advertisement, but usually refers to the descriptive text used to persuade you to buy the product or service.

Look at what is said about the product. Does it use any of the following?

Buzz words: These are used to make a product sound more attractive. They are usually jargon associated with the type of product but become vogue words. For example, in cosmetic advertising, buzz words such as 'dermatologically tested' and 'innovation' are often used. However in car advertising buzz words such as 'aerodynamic' and 'high performance' are common.

Superlatives: The use of words such as 'biggest', 'best', 'most powerful', 'fastest'.

Imperatives: These are words that give an order such as 'go', 'get', 'buy', 'order now'.

Rhetorical questions: Questions that do not require an answer: 'Are you tired of boring holidays?' 'Fed up with your old car?'

Pseudo-science: Technological jargon used to convince the target audience of the difference between this and other similar products.

Punctuation: Copy sometimes uses excessive aspects of punctuation such as exclamation marks to make the sentence sound more exciting!!!

Alliteration: Use of words that begin with the same letter. This poetic device is used to make phrases and slogans stick in the mind e.g. 'The wonder within'.

Puns: A play on words, it uses words or phrases that sound alike to use humour. Look at the sample answer on the Honda Marlin to see the use of puns.

Special offers: In order to grab attention special offers and discounts are often used.

SAMPLE ANSWER

Write a critical analysis of the advertisement which accompanies this examination paper. Your answer should deal with all the advertising techniques which you find in the text and visual of the advertisement.

(Junior Certificate, 1996)

Exam hint

Critical analysis does *not* mean to criticise. It means to carefully examine all aspects and comment on them. You may be completely positive or negative in your comments but a balanced answer is always better.

LAND A HONDA MARLIN. £99˚ A MONTH (APR 7.9%).

Honda are proud to announce the catch of the century.

The new Summer Edition Civic Marlin.

£9,880 on the road. And just £99˚ a month will reel it in for you.

And as for all the tackle you'll be getting, read on.

An electric tilt-and-slide sunroof, 16-valve engine, power steering, a driver's airbag,

ADVANTAGES PLUS	
Offer based on a maximum permitted mileage of 12,000¹	
Total cash price¹¹	**£9,880**
Deposit	£3,083
Amount of credit	£6,797
Deferred amount¹	£5,336.95
First payment¹¹	£149
23 normal monthly repayments¹	£99
APR 7.9%	
Total amount payable	£10,845.95
Guaranteed future value³	**£6,336.95**

double-wishbone suspension, a stereo radio cassette system, and of course, the appropriate summer graphics.

The Marlin is a car crammed with features from head to tail.

What's more, it doesn't drink like a fish. You'll be able to spot it in two colours, Captiva Blue Pearl and Tahitian Green.

With trim and both bumpers seamlessly

colour co-ordinated.

And as if all this wasn't enough, your Honda dealer has a little more bait. A year's free comprehensive insurance¹²

All the details can be found on the end of this line: 0345 159 159.

Go on, admit it. We've got you hooked.

(Er...that's enough fish jokes–Ed.)

THE NEW HONDA CIVIC MARLIN.

Key words

In this advertisement the product being advertised is the Honda Marlin car. There are many advertising techniques used in this advertisement to grab our attention and to focus on the positive aspects of the product. There are many associations made with an affluent lifestyle and a happy consumer. We will look at these techniques in more detail in both the visuals and the copy.

Visuals

In the visuals we see a happy, sun-tanned couple posing beside a Honda Marlin, which is held aloft as if it was a fish recently caught. As the name of the car, the Marlin, is also a fish this association makes sense. The colours used are predominantly blue; the light blue of the sky, the turquoise blue of the man's shirt and the darker blue of the car itself. These colours associate the product with the sea. They are also cool calming colours and so associate the product with both the strength and power of the sea and being calm, cool and collected.

The couple in the picture are linking arms, signifying closeness. They look to be in their thirties. They are tanned, wearing shorts and sunglasses and grinning broadly. The lifestyle that is associated with the product is therefore one of success and happiness. The target audience is young couples, probably without children. The setting is exotic and foreign: the blue sky, the sunset reflected in the car window, the piece of a palm tree on the right. All of these things associate the product with a jet-setting lifestyle. This is reinforced by the yachts in the background. The couple look very normal however. They are not air-brushed models and so represent the average consumer.

The logo for Honda is in the top left-hand corner. The red background contrasts with the sky and draws attention to the logo. The stylised H in the logo, with its angularity and strong vertical lines signify strength and power. These vertical lines are echoed throughout the visual, both by the masts of the yachts and by the vertical car itself.

The slogan 'Built without compromise', suggests the same strength and dependability despite the fun-loving theme that runs throughout the rest of the advertisement.

The fact that the car is hanging vertically is eye-catching and unusual. It also echoes the headline at the bottom of the visual 'Land a Honda Marlin'. This comparison between the car and a fish are continued in the copy.

Key words

Copy

Throughout the copy there are a series of puns on fish-related themes, carrying on the comparison made in the visual. These puns are like clichés or corny jokes throughout the copy e.g. 'will reel it in for you', 'from head to tail', 'it doesn't drink like a fish', 'All the tackle you'll be getting'.

The copy gives a list of all the extras with the car: 'tilt and shade sunroof', 'double wishbone suspension'. These buzzwords make the product seem more attractive and technologically advanced.

The copy also uses alliteration , 'colour co-ordinated', 'car crammed'. These are used to grab your attention.

The copy is also concerned with image and appearance. The car will have 'appropriate summer graphics', will be found in two colours continuing the nautical theme, 'Captiva Blue Pearl and Tahitian Green'.

The copy also uses imperatives 'Go on, admit it'. The use of parenthesis (brackets) at the end of the advertisement (er . . . that's enough fish jokes – Ed.) gives the advertisement an informal, fun-loving feel.

Overall the advertisement is well structured with the nautical theme carried through from the visuals to the copy. This links up with the name of the product, the Marlin. The lifestyle associated with the product is successful and fun-loving, but still looking for value for money. The target audience are looking for a fun car but are still concerned with safety. This advertisement successfully links all of these aspects of the product through its use of the nautical theme.

QUESTIONS

Examine the following advertisements and write a critical analysis for each.

A

B

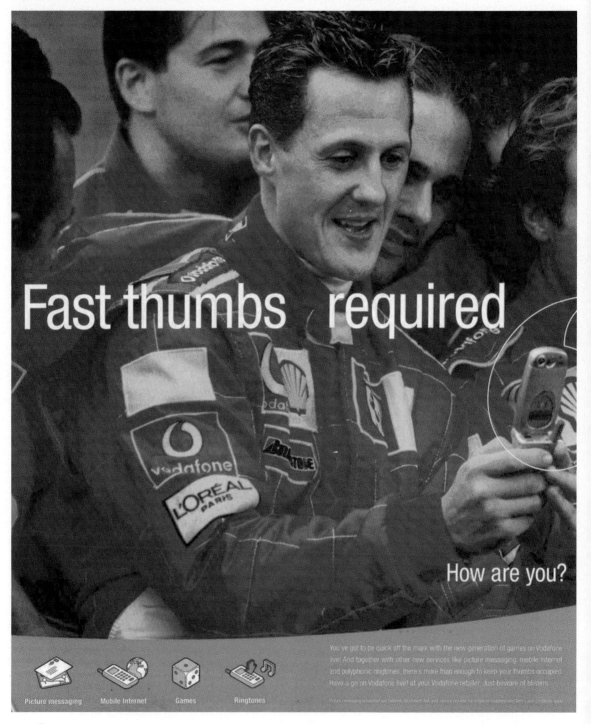

C

Newspapers

There are two main types of newspapers: tabloids and broadsheet. You need to be aware of the differences between these two types of newspapers.

Tabloids	Broadsheets
Smaller size	Large size
Sensationalist headlines	Factual/informative headlines
Large photographic content	More text, less photos
Block headlines	Longer articles
Human interest stories	Politics/world affairs/financial
Celebrity watching	Analysis of events
Paparazzi photos	Photo journalism

The main differences between these two papers can be seen in the layout of the front page of each. In the tabloid newspaper the front page is usually very colourful and eye-catching with a large photo dominating the page. Special offers, colour banner headline, reverse print (white print on black background) are all usually present. In a broadsheet newspaper the front page will often contain a number of stories on a variety of topics, one photo, usually in colour, and a large amount of densely packed text.

QUESTIONS

Look at the following examples of both tabloid and broadsheet newspaper front pages and examine how the news is reported in each.

1. How is colour used?
2. Can you find examples of sensationalist or emotive language in the tabloid headlines?
3. What other devices are used in the headlines to grab the attention of the readers?

THE IRISH TIMES

€1.50 (INCL. VAT) 75p sterling area. | Tuesday, October 26, 2004 | WWW.IRELAND.COM

HealthSupplement: 8 pages with top health jobs

Cancer survival: a better outlook

Turning the disabled into outcasts

Staffing crisis in boarding schools

EducationToday: 12-13

Jazz festival ends on high note

Ray Comiskey: 14

NewsDigest

Two Irish MEPs ready to reject new Commission

Labour's Mr Proinsias De Rossa and Sinn Féin's Ms Mary Lou McDonald have said they will vote against the appointment of the new European Commission in the European Parliament tomorrow unless Mr Rocco Buttiglione is moved to a different post: **page 7**

ESB operating profits expected to reach €375m

Despite rising fuel costs, the ESB is expecting to report an increased operating profit of approximately €375 million for 2004, although higher interest payments are likely to reduce the company's pre-tax performance: **page 18**

HomeNews

Road deaths: Six people were killed on the roads in the Republic during the Bank Holiday weekend, despite an increased Garda presence as part of the "Arrive Alive" road safety campaign: **page 5**

Dublin marathon record: Around 10,500 runners took part in yesterday's Dublin marathon, the biggest number since 1982. Lezan Kimutai (right) from Kenya won the men's race in a record time of 2 hours 13 mins 8 secs: **pages 3 and 23**

Beef reassurance: The Food Safety Authority of Ireland has moved to reassure consumers about the safety of Irish beef as a man continues to be treated in hospital in Dublin for suspected vCJD: **page 3**

BusinessNews

Elan settlement: Elan has reached a $75m settlement of the action taken by US shareholders and is to pay a $15m civil fine in relation to an investigation by the US Securities and Exchange Commission: **page 18**

Offer for Warner Chilcott: The Northern Irish speciality pharmaceuticals company said yesterday it had received a takeover offer of 837p a share, valuing the firm at about £1.57 billion (€2.26 billion): **page 18**

WorldNews

15 Palestinians killed: Israeli troops killed 15 Palestinians and wounded over 70 in a raid on the Khan Younis refugee camp, just hours before Prime Minister Sharon opened a debate in parliament on his withdrawal plan: **page 10**

Failure on EU asylum system: The Minister for Justice, Mr McDowell (left), and his EU Justice and Home Affairs counterparts have failed to agree on a five-year plan to create a common asylum and immigration system: **page 9**

SportsTuesday

International Rules: GAA president Seán Kelly said the series with Australia does not need to be seriously re-evaluated despite Ireland's record aggregate win by 50 points: **page 23**

Soccer: Arsenal could face FA charges after police officers saw one of their players pouring soup and pizza over Manchester United manager Alex Ferguson in the tunnel after Sunday's match at Old Trafford: **page 21**

Weather

It will be sunny and dry at first today with cloud and patchy rain spreading from the west. Highest temperatures 10-13 degrees. Freshening southeasterly winds later: **page 28**

Index

Home.......2-7	Opinion 16	Sport....21-26
World ,...9-11	Letters 17	Bulletin 28
Arts...........14	Finance 18-19	TV 30

THE IRISH TIMES 10-16 D'Olier Street, Dublin 2
Telephone: (01) 6758000
Fax: Newsdesk (01) 6772130. Sport 6799959.
Business 6798874. Advertising 6773241.
Online: **www.ireland.com**
The recommended retail price of **THE IRISH TIMES** in the Republic of Ireland is €1.50
THE IRISH TIMES has been named Best Printed National Newspaper by *Irish Printer* magazine.

9 771393 351024 44

Volume No. 47143. Tuesday, October 26, 2004

Democratic presidential nominee Senator John Kerry (left) and former US president Bill Clinton campaigning at a rally in Philadelphia yesterday. Photograph: Brian Snyder/Reuters

Clinton joins Kerry on campaign trail

CONOR O'CLERY
IN PHILADELPHIA

Making his first public appearance since heart surgery in September, former US president Bill Clinton campaigned with Senator John Kerry at a rally attended by tens of thousands in Philadelphia yesterday.

"From time to time they called me the comeback kid but in eight days John Kerry is going to make America the comeback country," said Mr Clinton, who received a tumultuous welcome from the crowd.

The former president, who looked pale and thin, will continue campaigning for Mr Kerry in Florida today. Later in the week he is expected to visit Nevada and New Mexico before travelling to his home state of Arkansas on Sunday, the Kerry campaign said.

Both Pennsylvania and Florida are among the most keenly fought battleground states in the election. Mr Kerry is slightly ahead in Pennsylvania and in a dead heat with President George Bush in Florida.

His strategic deployment in Philadelphia, a must-win state for the Democrats, was aimed at re-igniting the enthusiasm, especially among black voters that he inspired as president, and to get Democrats to turn out in sufficient numbers on polling day to defeat the Bush-Cheney campaign.

Speaking without a script, Mr Clinton peppered his speech with statistics. He reminded them that under Mr Bush America had lost jobs for the first time in 70 years.

Pennsylvania had lost 70,000 jobs, compared to the 219,000 gained "when that last fella' was in office". Since Mr Bush took office, 330,000 Pennsylvanians had lost their health care and 249,000 had been added to the poverty rolls.

Meanwhile, Mr Bush, with former New York mayor Rudolph Giuliani at his side, criticised Mr Kerry's strategy of "pessimism and retreat" and told voters in Colorado that "in every critical respect, my opponent and I see the war on terror differently. The choice is not only between two candidates – it is between two directions in the conduct of the war on terror.

"Will America return to the defensive, reactive mind set that sought to manage the dangers to our country? Or will we fight a real war with the goal of victory?"

Mr Giuliani, widely praised for his leadership in New York after the September 11th attacks, told the crowd that Mr Kerry "can't seem to make up his mind whether terrorism is serious or a nuisance". – *(Additional reporting Reuters)*

Clinton welcomed like returning star player: page 11
Editorial comment: page 17

After five days lost in Paris, Irishman calm and hungry

LARA MARLOWE
IN PARIS

Mr Brendan Brady, the disabled Irishman who disappeared at EuroDisney last Wednesday, was found by police, sitting on a park bench at the Rond-Point des Champs-Élysées in Paris at about 6.30 p.m. yesterday. He had gone missing during a visit to the theme park organised by RehabCare.

At the police commissariat of the 8th arrondissement last night, Mr Des North, the community services manager for RehabCare, was the first familiar face Mr Brady had seen since Wednesday.

"He was cool as a breeze," Mr North said. "I gave him a big hug. I'm sure I broke his ribs. He said he was feeling pretty good and I asked him if he needed a doctor. He said no, all he was was hungry. He wanted a cheeseburger and chips."

The first thing Mr Brady did was telephone his mother Eileen in Palmerstown, west Dublin. When Mrs Brady said: "Oh my God Brendan, I thought I'd never see you again!", Mr Brady replied: "I'm fine," and shrugged, calm in the midst of the bustle.

Mr Brady's clothes were grimy and he had five days growth of beard, but he seemed so fit that the RehabCare staff who had searched hostels, train stations and Irish pubs for him accepted he did not need a hospital. "I'm not walking anywhere else!" he said.

In a police commissioner's office, Mr Brady (42) told how he had absent-mindedly followed a crowd into Chessy train station last Wednesday, mistaking them for his group of 10 from RehabCare.

When he realised his mistake, he bought a train ticket back into the city. "I didn't sleep at all the first night," he said. He got into a taxi and asked for his hotel, but he could not remember the street.

For five days he walked, asking where the Kyriad Hotel was, not knowing that the chain has six hotels in Paris. An American befriended him as did several French people with good English. He meant to go to the police, but never got round to it.

He was found when three patrol officers, who had seen a television news report, and a policewoman recognised him from the posters RehabCare had placed in metro stations.

"Do you realise you're famous, Brendan?", his friends asked. "Ah yeah?" he replied, with the slightest chuckle. They showed him the missing poster. "That's not a great picture of me," he commented.

Cowen adopting 'conservative' stance on Budget

Minister warns Cabinet colleagues of limited scope for spending increases

ARTHUR BEESLEY,
POLITICAL REPORTER

Mr Cowen: health, social welfare and education to be priorities

The Minister for Finance, Mr Cowen, has adopted a "conservative" stance in negotiations with Ministers during the run-up to the publication next month of his first Budget Estimates.

As the Estimates campaign nears its conclusion, senior sources said Mr Cowen had indicated to his Cabinet colleagues that he would have limited scope to increase spending outside the priority areas of health, social welfare and education.

Any additional spending is likely to be reserved for the politically sensitive areas of community employment, Garda recruitment and the indexation of tax bands and credits, the sources said.

Mr Cowen is said to be forecasting a general Government deficit of 0.8 per cent of Gross Domestic Product in 2005 in the Book of Estimates, which will be published on November 18th.

This is less than the 1.1 per cent deficit forecast in the last budget by his predecessor, Mr Charlie McCreevy, although buoyant tax revenues this year have eased the borrowing requirement considerably.

The EU measurement of debt, which strips out the State's contribution to the National Pension Reserve Fund, currently indicates that the Exchequer may record a small surplus this year.

In advance of Budget day on December 1st, Mr Cowen will also hold a series of meetings with Fianna Fáil TDs and senators to hear their concerns.

While the Minister has insisted that he will not change the Government's economic policy, senior political sources believe there will be a shift of emphasis in favour of social spending.

However, despite the recovery in the public finances, Mr Cowen has warned Ministers that his room for manoeuvre will be constrained by three public pay increases set out in the latest phase of the Sustaining Progress agreement.

While the Tánaiste and Minister for Health, Ms Harney, is expected to secure a significant rise in health funding, political sources said pay costs would take up a large portion of the increase.

Mr Cowen's caution has been repeated by officials in the Department of Finance who have stressed in the negotiations that the rapidly increasing price of oil, the war in Iraq and twin deficits in the US have the potential to seriously undermine the performance of the domestic economy.

However, multi-million euro investment in areas such as transport will continue under the five-year capital spending plans introduced by Mr McCreevy in the budget last December.

Money not spent on capital projects this year will be brought forward for spending in 2005, although it will counted as expenditure in 2004.

With the Government seeking to redefine its image in the wake of its poor performance in the local and European elections, sources said Mr Cowen was likely to concentrate on commitments not met since Fianna Fáil and the Progressive Democrats agreed on the Programme for Government in 2002.

Chief among these is the promise to increase the strength of the Garda by 2,000, a commitment which was repeated in recent weeks by the Minister for Justice, Mr McDowell, when he announced a three-year recruitment programme.

Mr McDowell is considered unlikely to have pushed ahead with that initiative without a commitment on funding from Mr Cowen.

In addition, the new Minister for Enterprise, Trade and Employment, Mr Martin, has also signalled a renewed commitment to the community employment scheme, a subject of significant pressure within the Fianna Fáil parliamentary party.

On income tax, the Taoiseach, Mr Ahern, gave a clear indication a fortnight ago that Mr Cowen was examining the tax bands.

Any development in this area would see the Minister move towards the Government target of 80 per cent of all earners paying tax at the standard 20 per cent rate.

This has not been done in recent budgets, meaning more middle-income earners have been pushed into the higher rate band.

Given the pressure on the Government to change its "right-wing" image, Mr Cowen is also likely to increase tax credits to exempt more low earners from tax and provide a boost for all income tax payers.

With Home Start free
until November 12th,
there's never been
a better time to join the AA.

Call **1850 456 789** or buy online at **aaireland.ie.**

AA
ONE DAY...

The offer of Home Start applies for the first year only. Terms and conditions apply.

IRISH DAILY STAR

SUPPORTING JOBS IN IRELAND

NOW WE DO IT EVERY DAY

Tuesday October 26 2004
€1.20 (Inc vat)

9 771649 430022

Ruud in dock ...and it's war and pizza for Fergie
— SEE PAGES 70, 71 & BACK

MISSING: Puppy Brock

Help us find our Croke Park pooch

THE owners of the dog who had the nation in stitches when he invaded the Croke Park pitch on Sunday have appealed for help to find him.

The Byrne family from Ballyfermot, Dublin have been searching for their dog Brock since Friday and were shocked to see him on TV running around Croke Park.

The Jack Russell, who is just over a year old, eluded players and officials for eight minutes before being removed from the pitch — but the GAA were last night unable to say what had happened to him.

■ SEE PAGE 9

MIRACLE

Brendan found alive five days after he vanished in Paris

SAFE: Brendan Brady

HUGE RELIEF: Eileen (centre) and family celebrate the news

IRISHMAN Brendan Brady was found alive and well in Paris last night — five days after he went missing during a trip to Eurodisney.

His mother Eileen told *The Star*: "I can't believe it. It took a miracle to bring him back."

Physically handicapped Brendan (42) was found by a female police officer who noticed his face from public notices.

He had slept rough for five nights and survived on water and what he could buy with his meagre funds.

■ SEE PAGE 4

PARTS OF A NEWSPAPER

- Editorial – article by the editor expressing opinions on topical issues
- News reports – factual report on news items
- Feature article – discursive article on a topical issue
- Sports journalism – reporting and reviewing of sports events and news
- Letters to the editor – public response to items published or topical issues

- Entertainment – reviews about what's going on in cinema, theatre etc.
- Supplements: TV guide
  - Property
  - Farming
  - Appointments
  - Fashion

Read the following examples of journalism and answer the questions that follow.

MINE'S A SKINNY LATTE, DAHLING

A particular breed of woman frequents a certain upmarket coffee shop. Nikki Cummins puts on her David Attenborough hat and introduces *ladyus lunchus*

The ladies who lunch are a unique breed. With a code of behaviour, a style of dress and even a language all of their own, they are a law unto themselves and inhabit their own rarefied world. In a previous life I spent two years as a waitress in the café of a well-known department store. It allowed me a unique opportunity to observe this peculiar species: *ladyus lunchus*.

The ladies who lunched where I slaved had three things in common: they were bored, loaded, and chronically nosy. Oh yes, and they had no respect for the poor fools who bankrolled their vacuous existence. As often as not they were spending their husbands' money, but they had few inhibitions about loudly discussing the respective spouse's shortcomings. 'He's absolutely useless socially,' I overheard a perfectly manicured, well-coiffured blonde of an uncertain age exclaim to her coffee-drinking companions one day. 'If he's not talking about golf, it's football. What *did* they talk about before the ball was invented?'

She was only warming up. 'He's a social disaster. I'll never forget the time he asked Mary who Foie Gras was. He thinks that, because he came up the hard way, we all find his life story so fascinating. It's mind-numbingly boring. And, can you believe it, he even boasts about being a workaholic! A workaholic, for Christ's sake! He thinks that holding meetings all day and have a three-hour lunch makes him a workaholic. I wish he *was* a workaholic. At least he'd be kept out of the way!'

As the monologue went on I was slaving in front of a hot coffee machine, up to my eyes in frothy milk. Her companions were nodding sympathetically, cooing, 'I know, I know.' It was all very Sybil Fawlty.

Their attitude to their husbands wasn't unusual. These women seemed to have little respect for anyone or anything except the approval of their peers. As 'the help', I was neither to be seen nor heard – and, in most cases, not even directly addressed. Typical of the women was the vision in a full-length shearling coat who arrived in and instructed the ceiling, 'Yes, I'll have a low-fat cappuccino, no sprinkles.' Then she swished through the crowd, waving frantically, and said loudly, 'Dahlings, *there*

→

you are!' She joined her friends who had done exactly the same before choosing the only uncleared table, oblivious to the fact that I was there on my own, very clearly stressed and struggling to cope.

While they paid me no attention, I didn't envy the attention they paid to each other. It was hilarious to watch them scan each other, darting hidden glances from the hairdo down to the outfit, then to the shopping bags (only BT or an exclusive boutique would do). It was all very subtle, but they seemed to under-stand the code: the woman who looked the most expensively dressed and with the most expensive purchases would be deferred to by the others. They would part like the Red Sea to let her pass and smile knowingly at her; she would smile back apparently gratefully and humbly, all the while expecting it.

My other favourite customers were the brides who came for their complimentary champagne breakfast. To the untrained eye they appeared to be your mythical blushing virgins, but not far below the surface they were demonic control freaks who liked nothing better than to bark orders at an army of shop assistants. If this was war, then never was it more demonstrably futile. I found myself pitying their prospective husbands, probably nice, dutiful lads – you know, the sort that women like to bring home to mother.

The blushing bride-type loved to devour the shop assistants, treating them as mere snacks between their morning tea and their lunchtime green salad. My Bridezilla of the Year award went to one charmless lunatic who stamped her feet petulantly, shouting: 'I want my wedding to be perfect, perfect, *perfect!*'

I'm glad to say my waitressing days are behind me – at least for the moment, and fingers crossed. But in a strange way, I miss those ladies who lunched. And when I see one of the just-stepped-out-of-the-salon women walking down Grafton Street, Prada bag in hand, I can't help but imagine the dialogue when she sits down for coffee with her friends. 'Oh Sheila, he has my heart broken. He mixed up the wines again on Saturday night . . . '

There did come a time when I began feeling as I imagined David Attenborough must when observing the intricate social behaviour of primates. Perhaps he'd be interested in doing a show about it? Now that would be something to get your teeth into.

Nikki Cummins, *Sunday Independent*, 4 April 2004

QUESTIONS

1. How does the writer show her dislike of the ladies who lunch?
2. How is she treated by the ladies?
3. How does the writer show her dislike of the brides to be?
4. What do you think of this writer's style of writing? Give reasons for your answer.

ALL THE RAGE Rósín Ingle

4: Clamping rage

What is it? You've been running out all day to stick money in the meter and reckon all is well until 6pm. Wrong. When you get to the car you realise you have miscalculated – and within a minute of the meter running out a team of highly skilled clampers, trained to lie in wait for people like you, has fastened another yellow wheel lock on your car. They are just sticking that alarming 'Stop, Do Not Attempt to Remove!' sticker on the window when you arrive, panting, with only five minutes to collect your child from the crèche/pick up the dry-cleaning/ drive your sick grandmother to the hospital. For the third time this week you shell out €80 for the crime of being a bit forgetful. Clampers? More like Black and Tans.

The symptoms? They range from mumbling obscenities about where you would like to stick the banana-coloured trap to taking more drastic action. The worst reported case of clamping rage came from Finbar Onuke, a taxi-driver who two years ago emerged from the dental hospital in Dublin, where he was having a tooth extracted, to find his car double-clamped. Helped by a passing pedestrian, he removed one clamp and tried to drive off with part of the other one still attached. He was fined more than €2,000 for his trouble. Clamping rage doesn't pay.

The cure? Park in one of the three-and-a-half legal parking spaces still available in Dublin (there are rumoured to be about seven left in Cork and Galway), thus avoiding contact with the clampers. Otherwise you could try an appeal. There was uproar in Galway recently over the clamping of a car that was being used to drive a sick child to hospital. Clamping company Control Plus even apologised, which is not something you hear from the men in white vans every day. Mostly, though, you are in the wrong and they are in the right. You could always swap the car for a motorbike or a bicycle. They aren't authorised to clamp these modes of transport. Yet.

The Irish Times, 25 May 2004

QUESTIONS

1. What are the main points made by the writer?
2. What, do you think, is her attitude towards the clampers?
3. What type of reader is this article aimed at?

PRESSURE TO BE PERFECT: TEENS UNDER THE KNIFE

Louise Holden

'Already I have had a few parents looking to pay for boob jobs for their daughters as a reward for good marks in the Leaving Cert. These parents should know better.' Is cosmetic surgery for teenagers the latest US import?

MTV's *I Want a Famous Face* and US drama *Nip/Tuck* are just two of a raft of new television programmes focusing on cosmetic surgery. While surgical procedures to enhance physical appearance are not new, this is the first time that TV audiences have engaged so intimately with the processes and treatments available. But how are these images impacting on teenagers, who are more conscious of their appearance than any other group?

In the United States, cosmetic surgery is relatively common among teens, who often receive breast augmentation surgery or nose reshaping as graduation gifts. The quintessential US teen Britney Spears had her breasts enlarged aged 17. There is nothing like the same level of demand for plastic surgery from teenagers in Ireland, but growing awareness of the treatments available is starting to filter down to younger age groups.

According to a senior surgeon at the Irish Cosmetic Surgery Group, there has been a gradual increase in the number of Irish teens looking for treatments such as nose reshaping, breast augmentation and ear pinning.

'Teenagers are liable to get fixated on a certain part of their body, such as their ears,

COSMETIC SURGERY AND TEENS: SOME POINTS TO REMEMBER

- The most common procedure carried out on under-18s in Ireland is otoplasty, or ear pinning. It's straightforward but does involve a general anaesthetic.
- Reputable surgeons in Ireland are unlikely to agree to breast enhancement surgery for teens except in unusual circumstances, such as associated depression.
- Rhinoplasty (nose reshaping) is not recommended before age 18 in girls and age 19 in boys.
- Some Irish cosmetic surgery practitioners refuse to carry out any procedures on under-18s.
- If you decide to take your child for a consultation, research carefully first. Make sure that the surgeon you are dealing with is on the Medical Council's Specialist Register and has held a post in reconstructive surgery in a public hospital. If your first consultation is more like a sales pitch than a medical consultation, look elsewhere.

nose or breasts,' he says. They can drive parents up the wall looking for surgical procedures to correct what they see as a problem. Parents need to take a balanced approach when deciding whether or not to take the matter further. For some teens, their preoccupation with changing their ears or nose may pass like last year's demands for a PlayStation. For others, there could be a real issue that needs to be addressed.

The most common surgical procedure carried out on under-18s in Ireland is otoplasty to pin back prominent ears. This is a relatively straightforward intervention and

→

children as young as six years old have been known to present for treatment. In many cases, these children have suffered at the hands of bullies in school and parents are happy to take whatever measures are necessary to ease the child's passage through secondary school.

Surgeon Andy Skanderowicz of the Dublin Cosmetic Surgery Centre doesn't see much of an issue with carrying out otoplasty on young children who need it. Prominent ears are very common in Ireland, and can cause a great deal of misery for children.

He is not so universally approving on the subject of nose reshaping or breast augmentation, however.

'I have only carried out one breast augmentation on a 17-year-old and that was after extensive counselling with the patient and her parents,' says Dr Skanderozicz. 'In that case, the girl had no breast development at all and it looked likely that she wouldn't.' She was so self-conscious about her chest that she had stopped going to school on PE days and her parents were very concerned.'

Generally, however, Dr Skanderowicz dissuades teenagers from nose or breast reshaping. 'The body continues to change and grow into the late teens and early 20s. Cosmetic surgery that is carried out too early can result in distortion. The bones in the nose, for example, do not fully take shape until 18 years old in a girl and 19 in a boy. I do get requests from 14- and 15-year-olds for reshaping, but I put them off until they are older.'

Dr Skanderowicz has also had requests for fat-reduction surgery, or liposuction, from a number of teens and their parents, but he's not keen. 'Liposuction is not a treatment for obesity. It can provide adults with the kick start they need to change their lifestyle, but I would always recommend diets and exercise to teens before surgery.'

Enhanced teen role model Britney and the anatomically incorrect Barbie doll

Some cosmetic surgery centres in Ireland have a policy of refusing treatment to anyone under the age of 18. Louise Braham of the Harley Medical Group explains why

⟶

her company has taken this decision. 'Teenagers' bodies are still changing and we steer clear of any surgical interventions on under–18s, including ear-pinning. We are vehemently against these ridiculous programmes on television promoting procedures such as liposuction for teens.'

Helena Ashdown-Sheils, managing director of Advanced Cosmetic Surgery in Dublin agrees. 'Quite a few young girls come to us with their parents looking for breast enhancement. Legally we have to consult with them, but our surgeons will always tell them to wait until they are 18, if not longer. All these programmes coming from the US are giving young people ideas. Already I have had a few parents looking to pay for boob jobs for their daughters as a reward for good marks in the Leaving Cert. These parents should know better.'

There are situations where surgical intervention at a young age can enhance a child's self-esteem and remove a serious social or physical obstacle. Breast-reduction surgery, for example, can make a huge difference where uneven proportions are causing a girl physical pain and embarrassment. If your child comes to you with a request for plastic surgery, it's important not to dismiss them out of hand, says a senior surgeon at the Irish Cosmetic Surgery Group.

'Even if you are totally against the idea of cosmetic surgery, don't disregard the child's desires,' he says. 'Talk to them about their feelings. If they seem to be genuinely determined, research the area with them. Even going as far as a consultation might solve the issue. The surgeon is very likely to try and put the child off until he or she is older and they may put an end to the matter.'

Ashdown-Sheils is glad that many adults now have the confidence to address physical hang-ups that have inhibited them all their lives. She is not so happy about the quick-fix image of cosmetic surgery that is being portrayed on TV, however. 'Whenever I meet young girls these days who find out what I do for a living, they are quick to list the procedures they plan to get done – breast enhancement, liposuction and so on. I say the same thing to all of them – forget surgery and get some exercise.'

Irish Times, 15 June 2004

QUESTIONS

1. Outline the arguments for and against cosmetic surgery for teenagers, as discussed in the article.
2. How has the media had an influence on the desire for plastic surgery?

Magazines

There are various types of magazines aimed at a specific target audience. The content of the magazine and the layout used can indicate the audience targeted.

As with newspapers they can contain:

- Editorials
- Feature articles
- Interviews
- Reports
- Letters
- Reviews

As magazines are published weekly or monthly news is not a high priority. Magazines can also be specialist publications focusing on a specific group of people or a hobby or interest. The advertising in these magazines are reflective of the audience targeted, a magazine on football is not going to contain advertisements for cosmetics.

Questions

1. What type of audience is this magazine aimed at? Give reasons for your answer.
2. What aspects of the layout are designed to be eye-catching?
3. What type of advertisements do you think would be present in this magazine?

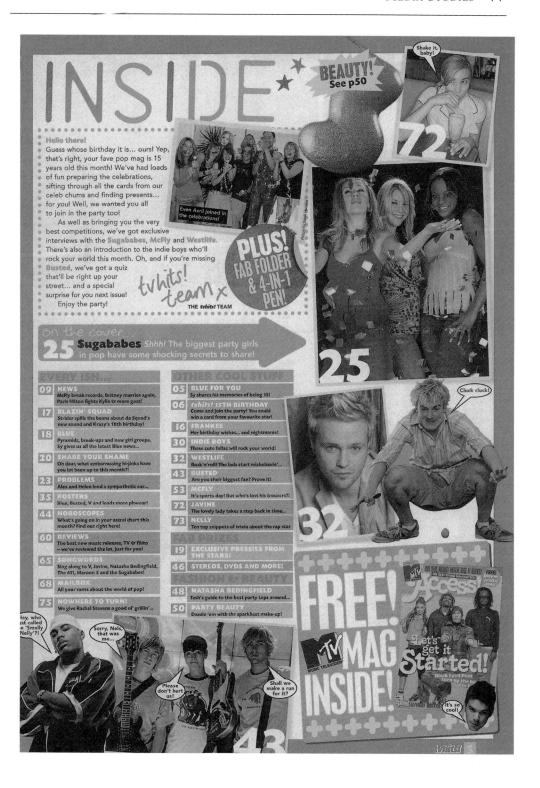

Cartoons

There are two types of cartoons found in the media: political and humorous.

PURPOSE

Political cartoons are there to make a satirical observation on the political situation. While often containing a humorous element they have serious undertones.

Humorous cartoons provide a social commentary or depict a comedic situation. Often they contain the same characters each week and are in serial format.

QUESTIONS

1. Who is the main character in the cartoon?
2. What point is being made by the cartoon?
3. What type of newspaper do you think this cartoon would appear in?

Television and Radio

Radio and television are the main forms of communications media used today. Almost every household has at least one television and its influence cannot be underestimated.

Your knowledge of this section of the media is quite broad because of your exposure to these forms of media throughout your life. However in terms of the exam there are key points and terms that you must familiarise yourself with in order to formulate your opinions on the topic.

RADIO

Radio in this country can be divided into two groups:
• National radio stations which broadcast nationwide.
• Local radio stations which have a limited broadcasting ability and focus on the needs of the local community which it serves.

National radio

National radio stations such as the state funded Radio 1, 2FM, Lyric and Radio na nGaeltachta along with the non-state funded national radio station, Today FM, have various things in common.

• They operate on a 24-hour basis.
• They must have news segments in each hour.
• They deal with national and international news and sporting events.
• They take live input from listeners via e-mail, telephone and text.
• They depend on advertising rates to fund the stations.
• They run competitions to boost listenership.
• They are DJ or personality based. They focus on specific DJs or personalities to give their station credibility and popularity. Therefore very popular DJs are paid quite well to encourage them to stay at a particular station.

Local radio

While some aspects of local radio are very similar to those for national radio, there are some differences.

• Local radio stations have some state funding to supplement advertising rates.
• Because they are based in a locality their news and sports reflect that locality. They deal with events that are of significance only to the locality where they

are broadcast, e.g. local deaths and mass times, running commentary on local sports events or interviews with local personalities.
• They don't always operate on a 24-hour basis but are limited to peak times.

QUESTION

Look at the following examples of schedules for a local and a national radio station. Examine the differences and similarities between the two formats.

RTÉ 2FM
FM: 90.4–92.2; 97 mHz.
6.00am The Full Irish. **7.00** The Full Irish **9.00** Gerry Ryan. **12.00** Gareth O'Callahan. **2.00** Michael Cahill. **5.00** Liam Quigley's Golden Hour. **6.00** Dave Fanning. **7.30** Newsbeat. **8.00** Countdown to '906'. **8.30** Rick O'Shea. **10.00** Jenny Huston. **12.00** Dan Hegarty. **2.00** 2FM Replay.

RTÉ LYRIC FM
FM: 96–99 mHz.
7.00am Lyric Breakfast. **10.00** Lyric Notes. Máire NicGearailt with music and features, including a reflection from Jim Norton, who has just recorded *Ulysses*, and music by Puccini. Artist of the week is Adreja Malir. **12.30** Summer Lunchtime Choice Concerts. Cathal Breslin (piano), RTÉ National SO/Peter Shannon. Mendelssohn: *Fingal's Cave*. Mahler: *Adagietto* (*Symphony No 5*). Prokofiev: *Piano Concerton No 1*. Bizet: *L'Arlesienne Suite No 1*. **3.00** The Full Score. Haydn: *Cello Concerto No 1 in C, H VIIb 1*. **5.00** Drivetime Classics. **8.00** Grace Notes. See Choice. **9.00** The Lyric Concert. See Choice. **10.30** The Blue of the Night. **1.00** Music Through the Night.

TODAY FM
FM:100–102 mHz.
7.00am The Ian Dempsey Breakfast Show. **10.00** The Ray D'Arcy Show. **1.05** Philip Cawley. **5.00** The Last Word. **7.00** Pet Sounds. **10.00** The Blast! – Ray Foley. **12.00** Small Hours – Donal Dineen. **2.00** Overnight Music.

NEWSTALK 106
FM: 106 mHz.
7.00am Breakfast with David McWilliams. **9.30** City Edition. **12.20** Lunchtime with Damien Kiberd. **2.30** Moncrieff. **4.30** The Right Hook with George Hook. **7.00** Off the Ball with Ger Gilroy: A preview of Holland v Germany. **10.00** Late Night Live.

RTÉ RAIDIO NA GAELTACHTA
FM: 92.6–94.4; 102.7 mHz.
6.00am Sé Bhur mBeatha. **7.00** Nead na Fuiseoige. **8.00** Adhmhaidin. **9.15** Scéal Aniar. **10.00** Príomhscéalta. **10.15** I gCeartlár na nDaoine. **11.00** Iris Samhraidh. **12.00** Príomhscéalta. **12.08** An Saol ó Dheas. **12.55** Tuairisc Spóirt. **1.00** Nuacht a hAon. **1.30** Glór Uibh Rathaigh. **2.00** Binneas Béil. **3.00** Seal Aduaidh. **4.00** Príomhscéalta. **4.08** Camchuairt. **5.00** Príomhscéalta. **5.55** Tuairisc Spóirt. **6.00** Nuacht a Sé. **6.30** An

Chaint sa Chathair. **7.00** Lán a' Mhála. **8.00** Glór na Mí. **8.30** Glór Uibh Ráthaigh. **9.00** Faoi do Chois é! **10.00** An Taobh Tuathail. **12.00** Scoth na Máirte.

RTÉ RADIO 1
FM: 88.2–90.0; 95.2 mHz, MW: 567, 729 kHz, LW: 252 kHz.
News on the hour. **5.30am** Risin' Time. **7.00** Morning Ireland. **9.00** Marian Finucane. **11.00** All Washed Up. With Cliona O'Carroll. 2: It Tosses Up Our Losses. **11.30** John Creedon. Incl. **12.00** *The Angelus*. **1.00** News. **1.45** Liveline. Conversation and phone-ins with Joe Duffy. To contact the show, call 1850 715 815 (ROI Callsave) or 0800 614 616 (UK Freephone). **2.45** Rattlebag. See Choice. **3.30** Brenda Power. **4.00** The Ronan Collins Show. **5.00** Five Seven Live. **7.00** The Tuesday Play. **7.30** The Future Tense. **8.00** Outside the Box. **8.30** The Mystery Train. **9.50** Nuacht. **10.00** Tonight with Vincent Browne. **11.25** The Book on One: *A Spring in My Step*, by Joan McDonnell. Read by Martina Carroll. **11.40** Today in the Oireachtas. **11.55** Sea Area Forecast. **12.00** Late Date. **2.00** Through the Night: Marian Finucane. **3.00** Liveline. **3.30** Five Seven Live. **4.00** Mystery Train. **5.00** All Washed Up.

CLARE FM		
6.30am	The Brighter Breakfast	Colum McGrath
8.30am	Sports Update	
8.35am	The Brighter Breakfast	Colum McGrath
10.00am	Summer Focus	Anne Slevin
12.00pm	Lunch Time Show	Pam Wilson
1.00pm	Lunchtime News	
1.20pm	Lunch Time Show	Pam Wilson
4.00pm	Pat Flynn's Drivetime	Pat Flynn
6.00pm	Main Evening News	
6.08pm	Pat Flynn's Drivetime	Pat Flynn
7.00pm	Reel Sound	Ita Kelly
9.00pm	Cormacology	Cormac MacConnell
12.00am	Midnight Stroll	Dara MacConnell
01.00–06.30am	Music Through the Night	Best Mix of music throughout the night

News on the hour, from 7am until midnight
Today's thought at 7.55am and 11.55am
Death notices at 8.04am, 9.04am, 1.20pm, 6.10pm, 10.05pm & midnight

Television

Television is probably the aspect of media you are most familiar with. The questions relating to television can be varied, relating to the effects of television, the scheduling or the types of programmes offered. Read the following article on reality television and answer the questions that follow.

IN REALITY IT'S CURTAINS, LET'S GO CELEBRATE

I have participated and have had fun. But sometimes I wonder what is lacking in viewers' lives that they keep on watching, ponders **Gavin Lambe-Murphy**

I guess I have appeared on more reality TV shows than most and to be honest, the only reason I did it was to see what it's all about. I wanted to see just what it was like to be locked away from the public with a group of total strangers rather than be surrounded by familiar faces and endless party invitations.

Well, despite what you may think, it is a very enjoyable experience – it was for me anyway. I was never one to shy away from a challenge and I like the idea of meeting up with new people and seeing what makes them tick. But after being one of the guinea pigs on three different reality shows – *Spoilt Young Posh and Loaded* (ITV1), *Celebrity 5 Go Dating* (Channel 4) and of course *Celebrity Farm* (RTÉ1) – I feel that I have done my share of reality television.

And perhaps the public has had its fill – of reality shows that is, not of me.

But it would be wrong of me to say it was a wasted experience. Maybe I was lucky to get the chance to do three totally different shows, but I found it interesting to realise how I changed throughout the course of the shows.

It most definitely was a learning experience – about myself.

But I also learned a lot about other people too – I suppose there may, after all, be something in the notion (put forward by the producers of *Teen Big Brother*) that these reality shows can sometimes be filed under educational programmes. Why shouldn't studying people in a controlled environment teach us as much as observing animals?

The people I met on my reality television circuit were all very different. Take the *Young Posh* show. In this environment the theory was that I was going to interact with a group of people who were very similar to myself.

But as it turned out, I couldn't stand any of them!

On the other hand the boys with whom I shared a flat in *5 Go Dating* proved to be really fun people and they are all now friends of mine. They were all so different and up for a laugh, which I think is the most important quality that a person can have.

Then, of course, there was *Celebrity Farm*. I have no reason to draw a veil over it, but let me just say that it was, by far, the most bizarre experience of the lot.

I have now come to the same conclusion as the rest of the nation. I am rather tired of reality television and feel that if I have to see another out-of-work celebrity punish his or her career further, I will go crazy.

We've had every posh twit from my good self to Paris Hilton to Henry Brock (my cousin); from Tara Palmer-Tomkinson to Lord Freddie Windsor appearing on the small screen.

Enough is enough!

And after *Big Brother, The Salon, Celebrity Fat Club, The Simple Life, Rich Kids, Rich Girls* the list should cease. I enjoyed them as much as anyone else – both participating and viewing. And you could say it gave some people a chance to show a talent that might otherwise have remained undiscovered. It was a pleasure to see Kerry McFadden shine like a star on *I'm a Celebrity, Get Me Out of Here*.

She was herself and the fact is, like most things in life, if you are yourself people recognise that and usually appreciate it.

But reality shows were of their time. It was a very short time in the great scheme of things and it must now be recognised that having come, that time is now gone.

But that is probably too much to hope for and I can only give one piece of advice to future participants – enjoy it. Try not to take it too seriously. There is a shared view by nearly all the other contestants I have met – it's a good laugh.

Afterwards can be a different matter. Dealing with new-found fame is not easy and can be the biggest pitfall for the ex-reality-show star. One day you are just a guy on the street buying a cup of coffee and the next, people want your autograph. Luckily for me, my face has been in so many publications and on television networks that it was a gradual thing.

I am still left with one final thought. What exactly is it that is lacking in so many people's lives that they feel the need to watch reality shows?

Sunday Independent,
22 February 2004

STARS BREED STARS ON TV

We've reality shows about reality shows. What next? Fiction TV? asks **Brendan O'Connor**

The *Littlest Groom* is apparently getting a rather small audience, which is fitting really given that it is based on small people. Midget love apparently isn't a winner in the ratings. Or maybe, perish the thought, people are getting tired of reality TV. We've come a long way from the first *Big Brother*. Now we've got everything from *Who Wants to Marry My Dad?* to *Second Chance: America's Most Talented Senior*, which manages to mix reality TV with political correctness.

In between we've got *Looking for Love: Bachelorettes in Alaska*, *Trading Moms* and *But the Sex is So Good*. I know several people who are addicted to the live operations they show late at night on Discovery Channel. And if that's not gory enough for you, then try the even bloodier car crash that is *The Simple Life* which features Nicole Richie and Paris Hilton tottering around small town America in high heels and hotpants.

You can see why TV companies are keen on the reality thing. The participants

→

generally don't become celebrities until the show airs so while the show is being made there are no hissy fits or big fees or Winnebagos. Also, reality shows are pretty much a banker. You could make 10 sitcoms before you'd hit on a formula that would find favour with the general public, but reality shows pretty much all work, however uninspired. Some of them even become bona fide classics that capture the public imagination in the way that no fictional show can. The most recent *I'm a Celebrity, . . . Get Me Out of Here* was almost a force of nature, a television phenomenon the like of which we haven't seen since JR was shot, or since *Celebrity Big Brother 2*.

You can see how the public like it as well. It's soap with the edge, the edge being that it's real and unpredictable. Why have a life yourself when you watch other people not having a life? Also we've turned on celebrities pretty badly over the last few years. The sheer magnitude of the publicity machine and the volume of entertainment media means that we know too much about celebs these days and that familiarity is obviously breeding contempt. So the notion of watching something that doesn't involve pampered celebs who live in a parallel universe was quite appealing. And of course when they did involve celebs

in reality TV it was generally down-on-their-luck has-beens so we enjoyed that too.

But you know, we hate to be taken for granted. Creativity was never a strong point with TV execs but at this stage they're not even pretending anymore. 'We need a new show. Let's do a reality show. Let's make it about dating. They can get married at the end. No, we've done that. OK, let's make them midgets, dwarves, little people, whatever they call them now.' It's only a matter of time before they base a show around trying to get John Waters's black lesbian whales to get married.

The innocence is gone out of it all too. There was a time when people went into the *Big Brother* house not quite knowing what to expect when they came out. Now the various wannabes know the grammar of reality TV inside out. They sit around the houses speculating on what kind of offers will be waiting for them on the outside world. These days your average contestant is more calculating than a hundred Nasty Nicks.

Inevitably we now have post-modern reality shows too, reality shows about reality shows. *Beyond Reality*, running on Channel 5, features the stars of reality shows in a reality show. Apparently the makers of *Big Brother* are thinking of suing because the show bears such a resem-

blance to *Big Brother*. Because people in a house was such an original idea in the first place.

A reality show of reality shows was bound to happen. It was one answer to the peculiar dilemma of what to do with the 'stars' of reality shows. TV people were clearly frustrated that they were creating stars that they were subsequently unable to capitalise on. The only thing they were good at was being in a reality show. The solution? Put them in another reality show. It's presumably only a matter of time before we start seeing professional reality show contestants, minor celebrities whose only claim to fame is that they are very good at appearing in reality shows. In fact the coughing major from *Who Wants to Be a Millionaire?* is well on his way to becoming one. He's already done a celebrity wife swap with Jade Goody, starred in a documentary about himself and now he's in *Beyond Reality*. Presumably he'll pop up again this time next year on *Beyond Reality – One Year Later, The Reunion* and then again in five years' time on *Whatever Happened to the Stars of Beyond Reality*. Interesting title *Beyond Reality*. Interesting because most TV people don't seem to be able to see beyond reality. And what is there beyond reality anyway? Fiction maybe?

Sunday Independent,
22 February 2004

QUESTIONS

1. What, according to the writers, is the appeal of reality television?
2. Would you agree with their analysis? Give reasons for your answer.
3. Are there any good points in favour of this type of programme?

TELEVISION SCHEDULES

Examine the following schedules and answer the questions which follow.

morning/afternoon   **may 1**

RTÉ1
3.50 Euro News *28179994* 8.10 Who Wants to Live Forever? *70312826* 8.35 Floyd's India *31211807* 9.05 UEFA Stories The best moments from the 1992 European Championships. *99899284* 10.00 Film Genre Epics (Followed by RTÉ News) *14774265* 11.00 Bergerac An eccentric old lady's past is tied to a sunken ship. (Followed by RTÉ News and Weather Forecast) *13754401* 12.00 The Irish RM *37399604* 1.00 RTÉ News (Followed by Weather Forecast) *37234371* 1.25 Saturday Matinee: Murder She Wrote: A Story to Die For (2000) Angela Lansbury. During a visit to Los Angeles Jessica Fletcher solves the killing of a former KGB officer. (Followed by RTÉ news and Weather Forecast) *25704642* 3.10 Welcome to Europe Highlights of EU Enlargement celebrations from Warsaw and Berlin. *35149401* 4.20 Eurovision Preview Marty Whelan looks ahead to this year's Eurovision Song Contest. *35445536* 4.50 Nuacht RTÉ (Followed by News for the Deaf) *48368642*

RTÉ NET2
6.35 The Den Weekend: Yumee *84138371* 6.45 Animals of Farthing Wood *20516468* 7.10 Mattimeo: A Tale of Redwall *14829449* 7.35 Let's Animate *56525371* 8.00 The Disney Club Children's cartoon and magazine show, featuring *Disney's 101 Dalmatians, Disney's House of Mouse, Kim Possible* and *Disney's Hercules. 14378642* 9.35 The Mummy *53809975* 10.00 Mary Kate and Ashley: In Action *59142604* 10.25 Mental Block *30337826* 10.40 Power Rangers: Wild Force *25650569* 11.05 Renford Rejects *75263642* 11.30 Seriously Weird *65854623* 12.00 Uroheroes With Europe becoming ever larger, Slovenian Emmanuel shares his unique take on his own nationality. *92302333* 12.15 Cartoon Time *71149420* 12.30 Totally Spies *30340333* 12.55 Smallville *45199536* 1.50 Champions League Magazine *46401791* 2.20 Sports Monthly *23685046* 2.50 AIB Rugby Tom McGurk presents live coverage of the semi-final of the AIB league. Shannon v Belfast Harlequins

live from Thomond Park. *51318517* 4.50 Radical Highs *40028438*

TG4
7.00 Euronews *13780826* 9.00 World of Wildlife *18184623* 9.30 World Sport Special *373301449* 10.00 Spórt Extreme (OS) *16148807* 10.30 On the Limit Sports *18180807* 11.00 Aussie Rules Highlights from the Aussie Rules League 2004. (Repeat) *13789197* 12.00 Cúla 4 *90153024* 12.03 Spongebob Squarepants *92306159* 12.15 Brothers Flub *79053913* 12.40 Mucha Lucha *23515826* 1.00 Kong *81599371* 1.20 Bás agus Olcas *27475975* 1.30 Justice League *37304536* 2.00 UBOS *37180456* 2.25 Seo Agaibh Mimi *35689389* 2.45 Angela Anaconda *73124081* 3.00 Spongbob Squarepants *67721333* 3.10 Samurai Jack *78314371* 3.35 Lizzie McGuire *33271888* 4.00 Pop 4 Interactive chart music show featuring the latest top 40 singles chart, competitions and the hottest videos. Presented by Siobhán Ní Cheallaigh. (Repeat) *65831772*   ➜

TV3

8.00 Emmerdale *18192642*
8.30 The Best of Ireland AM *26525807* **10.00 Go Racing** *13767975* **10.30 Go Doc** *65848062* **11.30 On the Limit Sport** *65849791* **12.00 Emmerdale Omnibus** Robert tries to convince Katie of his feelings. Shadrach has a hot date but hopes of romance end in disaster – and he gets his punishment in court. *18779791* **3.00 Coronation Street** Sally's stage dreams are shattered when Rosie turns her drama into a crisis. *56171913* **3.30 Coronation Street** Fiz squares up to Cilla, but is she a match for her scheming mother? Sparks fly when Ashley meets Claire's mother for the first time. *80501739* **4.00 VIP** Val faces up to a crooked DA who is trying to salvage his reputation by sending an innocent man back to prison. With Pamela Anderson. *65862642*

BBC1

6.00 Teletubbies *5386284* **6.40 Angelmouse** *9576130* **6.45 Clifford the Big Red Dog** *2809710* **7.00 Metalheads** *7927130* **7.15 Super Duper Sumos** *7946265* **7.35 Arthur** *2521081* **8.05 Fairly Odd Parents** *1063230* **8.30 The Saturday Show** *64197* **10.00 The Mysti Show** *46081* **11.00 Top of the Pops Saturday** *33517* **12.00 BBC News; Weather** *1273130* **12.10 Football Focus** *1464307* **1.00 Grandstand** *50777994* **1.05 Racing from Haydock** (1.10 Live) *48405178* **1.20 World Snooker Championship**

48419371 **1.35 Racing from Haydock** (1.40 Live) **1.50 World Snooker Championship** Further semi-final coverage. *84929230* B (2.10 Live) *45537130* **2.05 Racing from Haydock** (2.10 live) **2.20 World Snooker Championship** *33164888* **2.45 Irish Cup Final** Coleraine v Glentoran. Kick-off at 3.00. *33640333*

BBC2

6.00 Weekend 24 *8314772* **10.00 Saturday Kitchen** *26913* **11.30 Gary Rhodes: The Cookery Year** *4246* **12.00 World Snooker Championship** (Live) Steve Davis and John Parrott present further coverage from the semi-final at the Crucible in Sheffield. *4927265* **12.45 See Hear** The difficulties of deaf and hard of hearing people accessing NHS services. *5134081* **1.30 What the Romans Did for Us** The innovations and inventions brought by the Romans to Britain. *56025064* **1.40 FILM: Second Chance** (1953, Thriller) Starring Robert Mitchum and Linda Darnell. *7306449* **3.00 Talking Movies** Film News with Tom Brook *8867449* **3.25 FILM: Heaven Knows, Mr Allison** (1957, Drama) Romantic drama about a Roman Catholic nun and a hard-bitten US Marine stranded together on a Japenese-occupied island in the South Pacific during World War 11. Starring Deborah Kerr and Robert Mitchum. *75189739*

UTV

6.00 GMTV *3203555* **9.25 Ministry of Mayhem** *74795284*

11.30 CD:UK *76265* **12.30 ITV News; Weather** *38200536* **12.35 UTL Live News and Weather** *38200536* **12.40 On the Ball** Matt Smith, Clive Allen and Jim Beglin preview the weekend's Premiership action, including Manchester City v Newcastle, Charlton v Leicester, and Wolves v Everton. *7098994* **1.15 Quincy, ME** Asten forces Quincy to take some vacation time and brings in a temporary replacement and a personality clash ensues. *293449* **2.15 Coronation Street Omnibus** Todd gets a warning from Gail, and Eileen resorts to drastic action – which only serves to fuel his anger. The pressure is on. Rosie and Sally's dreams are shattered. With Bruno Langley *10329555*

CHANNEL 4

6.05 The Hoobs *1182159* **6.30 The Hoobs** *1423130* **6.55 The Great Adventure Race** *1433517* **7.25 Kwik-Fit Pirelli British Rally Championship 2004** *7886975* **7.55 Trans World Sport** *8090284* **8.55 The Morning Line** *1431081* **9.55 T4: Smash Hits Chart** *9891517* **10.25 T4: Newlyweds** *6929826* **10.55 T4: Friends** *9073449* **11.25 T4: Friends** *5374081* **11.55 T4: The OC** *3484265* **12.55 As If** *7084791* **1.30 Channel 4 Racing from Newmarket and Uttoxeter** (Live) The 1.40, 2.15. 2.55 (UltimateBet 2000 Guineas) and 3.30 races from Newmarket, and the 1.55 and 3.40 races from Uttoxeter. *466791* **4.00 FILM: The Mirror Crack'd** (1980, Crime) Starring Elizabeth Taylor and Rock Hudson. *9333*

QUESTIONS

1. What type of audience are the early morning programmes aimed at? Give examples.
2. Do you notice any difference between the stations in relation to news coverage?
3. How well are sports programmes distributed?
4. What would you change and why?

5
Drama

Section 1, Paper 2

The Drama section of the exam paper Section 1, Paper 2 is worth sixty marks – thirty marks for your answers on an unseen extract from a play and thirty marks for your answer on the play you have studied.

In the unseen section you have two options: Shakespearean drama and non-Shakespearean drama. You may answer either extract regardless of whether you have studied Shakespeare for your exam.

Exam Hints for the Unseen Drama

- Make sure you read the extract carefully.
- Take note of any introduction to the piece or explanations given. They may be very relevant to the questions asked.
- Familiarise yourself with the key characters. Make sure you know exactly what happens in the extract. Read it several times to make sure you understand all of it.
- Look at the relationships as revealed in the extract. How do the characters speak to each other? What is left unsaid?
- Read the stage directions. They often give indications as to the relationships between the characters and the underlying emotions.
- If you are familiar with the play from which the extract is taken, only refer to the extract in your answer.
- Read the questions and then re-read the extract to pick out key quotations to use in your answers.
- Read the questions carefully. Take note of sections in the question and structure your answer accordingly.

Key Elements of Drama

Throughout both sections you are expected to recognise and evaluate some basic aspects of drama. As with your study of fiction there are basic elements such as plot, characters, conflict and resolution that make a story interesting. With drama the way these aspects are portrayed are slightly different.

CHARACTERS

You should know, in detail, the main characters in the play you have studied (and be able to spell their names correctly!). Characters reveal aspects of their personalities through the things they do (their actions) and the things they say. Other perspectives may also be gained by looking at what other characters say about them in their absence. Playwrights give the actors an indication of what they intended of the character through stage directions. Quite often the fact that a line is intended to be delivered in a whisper will give it a different intention than if it was shouted across the stage.

In the play you have studied look at the types of characters that are present. Is there an obvious hero/heroine? And if so, an equally obvious villain? Or is there a pair of star-crossed lovers? Are family relationships dominating the action of the play and if so are the relationships depicted stereotypical? Or are they unusual, supportive or destructive?

Which characters have power? How do they get it? Through respect or fear? Does the balance of power shift throughout the play? Why? Who benefits? Who loses out?

You should know at least three characters in detail from the play you have studied and you should be able to answer the following questions on each.

Study plan

1. What is the first impression we get of this character? Think about the opening scene, costume, entrance and the first words.
2. What does he/she say that reinforces that impression or changes that impression?
3. Describe a key event which occurs during the play which affects that character.
4. How does the character react to this event? Actions? Quotes?
5. How does the character relate to others in the play? Give examples.
6. Does the character face a moment of crisis? How does the character deal with it?
7. What happens to this character at the end of the play? Has justice been served?

8. Has the character changed during the play? How? Why?
9. Does this character contrast with any other character? How?

PLOT

Like any story the drama you study will have a basic structure – a beginning, a middle and an end. You need to know the outline of the plot, the main sequence of events and how any conflict is resolved at the end.

To begin your study of the play you need to look at the opening scene.

Opening scene
1. What stage directions are given about the placement of the set on stage? Where and when is the play set?
2. Which character opens the play? What is his/her significance?
3. Which other characters enter in the opening scene?
4. How does their entrance change the momentum of the play?
5. What themes are introduced? (Love, hate, power etc.)
6. What elements of conflict are introduced in this scene?
7. How does this scene relate to the rest to the play?

Key moments
You also need to be able to identify key moments throughout the rest of the play. You may be asked to identify moments of sadness, conflict, passion, humour, drama, etc.

For each of these moments you should be able to:

- Describe the scene where this moment takes place: characters present, location and atmosphere.
- Describe what happened before the scene that led to this moment.
- Explain how the moment is sad, passionate, humorous, dramatic or shows conflict.
- Describe how this moment affects the various characters involved for the rest of the play.
- Describe how this moment affects the action of the rest of the play.

Resolution
The end of the play is usually where all loose ends are tied up and all conflicts are resolved. You may be asked to evaluate the end of the play as a resolution.

- Have all events satisfactorily led up to this point?
- Are all loose ends tied up?
- Has the sub-plot added to or detracted from the overall story?

THEMES

In all plays themes are dealt with in varying depth. You need to identify the main themes touched upon in the play you have studied and analyse the way these themes are treated.

Some of the main themes that you may come across are:

- Good v evil
- Love
- Prejudice
- Power
- Racism
- Greed
- Familial relationships

How are these themes explored by the play?
Do certain characters represent various opinions?
How are the themes resolved at the end of the play?

ATMOSPHERE

The atmosphere in the play is created by a combination of elements.

- The place where the play is set can add to the creation of atmosphere, e.g. an austere conservative castle, a wild untamed moor.
- The playwright may also use elements of nature to evoke an atmosphere of anticipation or suspense, such as a storm or flashes of lightning. Could these things represent the metaphorical turmoil on stage?
- The suggestion of the supernatural: ghosts, prophecies or strange noises can heighten the atmosphere on stage.
- Be aware, as you watch a production of a play, of the various elements used by the director which are external to the script to change the mood or atmosphere.

LANGUAGE

Look at the type of language used by the playwright.

- Is the play written a long time ago and use words that are no longer used (archaic words)?
- Does the play contain abbreviations that are commonly used?
- Does the play use colloquialism (the words and phrases used in a locality)?
- Is the play set in a place that has a specific accent and is the script written in that accent?

Aspects of Production

Particularly in the unseen section, you may be asked to comment on aspects of staging an extract of a play. The following headings may help you structure your answer.

STAGE SET

If you have seen any dramatic productions you will realise that there are many different ways a drama can be staged. The one that you may be most familiar with is the traditional stage. Usually square in shape with one side open to the audience, fronted by a proscenium arch. The sides of the stage contain wing space that allows for pieces of set to be moved on and off stage. They often have curtains at the front, which are closed at the end of the performance. While planning a set design a set designer will build a set box, which is a scaled down model of the design to ensure that all aspects of the set will function in the space allowed.

Another method of staging a production is in the round, which places the stage space in the centre and the audience on all sides. With this style of staging there are limitations as regards wing space and the movement of the set.

The black box set is another method of staging. This minimalist style removes all structural features of the stage by covering them in black. Items of set are suggested rather than represented on the stage. Many more modern plays use this style.

While designing a stage set or suggesting a set for the exam question bear the following points in mind:

- Remember the purpose is to suggest a time and a place where the action takes place. What are the vital elements? What is mentioned in the script?
- The set must be seen by the audience, so don't place items behind each other where they will not be seen.
- On the traditional stage you must consider what will be on the back wall of the stage as a backdrop.
- Large items of furniture (e.g. tables, chairs, mirrors etc.) can denote a sense of place.
- Smaller items such as pens, books and telephones that are handled by the actors are props rather than set.

LIGHTING AND SOUND

A sense of time and place can also be created using lighting and sound effects.

Strobe: A storm can be created using strobe lighting and thunder sound effects. Strobe lighting can also be used to create a sense of disjointedness on stage.

Colour: A change in lighting colour can be used to change the atmosphere on stage. For example, a blood red sky over Macbeth's castle creates a sense of foreboding. A marshy bog-land can be created using a mixture of green lighting and dry ice pumped onto the stage.

Gobo: A gobo is a metallic disk that is placed over a light on stage. Any pattern etched onto the disk will be cast onto the stage. This is often used to create the illusion of light through leaves or of light coming through a window. A rotating gobo can create an illusion of movement.

Effects: Various sound effects are often used in dramatic productions, from a phone ringing to a train arriving at the station. These effects can enhance atmosphere and eliminate the necessity for some elements of set.

Music: Music can be used to provide atmosphere or portray a mood. Any type of music can enhance a scene and give the audience a sense of anticipation.

COSTUME

One of the main aspects of stagecraft that defines a character for an audience is costume. What a character wears gives the audience an indicator as to their personalities. Think carefully about assigning costumes to characters from an unseen text.

- What do we learn about their personalities?
- In which era is the play set?
- Are there any clues in the introduction as to the time/place in which the play is set?
- Deal with each character from head to toe.

> **Hairstyle:** Long, straight, curly, coiffured, straggly, crew-cut, hippie, sleek, slicked back, etc.
>
> **Clothes:** Use adjectives! For example:
> - Blue, torn, ragged coat with worn patches.
> - White, starched, frilled blouse with a high collar.
> - Period costume, velvet dress with corseted waist, flowing train and heavily embroidered.
>
> **Shoes:** Boots, stilettos, trainers etc.
>
> Think also about accessories and props such as handbags, briefcase, doll, toy.

Shakespearean Drama

The following extract (in edited form) is taken from *A Midsummer Night's Dream* by William Shakespeare. Read the extract carefully and then answer the questions which follow.

A scene from
A Midsummer Night's Dream

> **Background to this extract:**
> - **Helena** loves **Demetrius.**
> - Demetrius loves **Hermia.**
> - Hermia loves **Lysander.**
> - Hermia and Lysander are to meet in the woods and run away to be married.
> - Helena informs Demetrius of this.
> - Helena hopes Demetrius will forget about Hermia and give his love to her.

Enter Demetrius, Helena following him.

Demetrius: I love thee not, therefore pursue me not.
Where is Lysander, and fair Hermia?
The one I'll slay, the other slayeth me
Thou told'st me they were stol'n unto this wood
And here am I, and mad within this wood
Because I cannot meet my Hermia.
Hence, get thee gone, and follow me no more.

Helena: You draw me, you hard-hearted adamant![1]

Demetrius: Do I entice you? Do I speak you fair?
Or rather do I not in plainest truth
Tell you I do not, nor I cannot love you?

Helena: And even for that do I love you the more.
I am your spaniel; and Demetrius,
The more you beat me I will love you.
Use me but as your spaniel: spurn me, strike me,
Neglect me, lose me; only give me leave,
Unworthy as I am, to follow you.
What worser place can I beg in your love
(And yet a place of high respect with me)
Than to be used as you use your dog?

Demetrius: Tempt not too much the hatred of my spirit;
For I am sick when I do look on thee.

Helena: And I am sick when I look not on you.

Demetrius: You do impeach[2] your modesty too much,
To leave the city and commit yourself

[1] magnet
[2] put in danger

Into the hands of one who loves you not;
To trust the opportunity of night,
And the ill counsel of a desert place.

Helena: Your virtue is my privilege: for that
It is not night when I do see your face,
Therefore I think I am not in the night;
Nor doth this wood lack worlds of company,
For you in my respect, are all the world.
Then how can it be said I am alone
When all the world is here to look on me?

Demetrius: I'll run from thee and hide me in the woods
And leave thee to the mercy of wild beasts.

Helena: The wildest hath not such a heart as you.

Demetrius: I will not stay thy questions. Let me go;
Or if thou follow me, do not believe
But I shall do thee mischief in the wood.

Helena: Ay, in the temple, in the town, the field,
You do me mischief. Fie, Demetrius,
Your wrongs do set a scandal on my sex!
We cannot fight for love, as men may do;
We should be wooed, and were not made to woo.

Exit Demetrius

QUESTIONS

1. What kind of relationship is evident between Demetrius and Helena? Support your answer by reference to the text.
2. For a classroom production of this scene you have been chosen to play the part of Demetrius or Helena. How would you play your part? You might refer to tone of voice, movement, costume and facial expression.
3. Basing your answer on evidence from the text, would you like either Demetrius or Helena as a boyfriend or girlfriend? Support your answer by reference to the text.

(Junior Certificate, 2002)

Hint
Pick out key words in the question and make sure you focus on these words. Divide your answer into paragraphs.

SAMPLE ANSWERS

Only *two* of the following answers are necessary.

Q1. What kind of relationship is evident between Demetrius and Helena? Support your answer.

Plan: **Relationship**
–   not normal
–   D hates H, makes him sick
–   H no respect
–   lack of equality

The relationship depicted is not a normal, loving relationship. While it is clear that Helena loves Demetrius, *'And even for that I do love thee more'*, it is equally obvious that Demetrius has no feelings for her, *'I love thee not'*.

Demetrius wants to be rid of Helena and sees her presence as a hindrance, *'get thee gone, and follow me no more'*. He is very forthright and adamant about his feelings. He clearly tells her that he doesn't love her, in fact he is sickened by her presence, *'I am sick when I do look on thee'*. Yet he in some way still respects her and warns her not to put herself in danger, *'You do impeach your modesty too much'*. Yet when she fails to heed his warning he has no problem running away from her and leaving her *'to the mercy of wild beasts'*.

Helena seems to have no self-respect. She begs Demetrius to allow her to follow him like a dog, *'use me but as your spaniel'*. She twists his words to show the depth of her love, *'and I am sick when I look not on you'*. She pleads and flatters him, *'it is not night when I see your face'* and yet insults him when she doesn't like his response, *'the wildest hath not a heart such as you'*.

When Demetrius exits she is determined to follow him even though she admits that as a woman, *'we should be wooed, and were not meant to woo'*. The inequality in their relationship is evident as is the difference in their feelings for each other. Overall their relationship is not equal, not stable and not normal.

Q2. For a classroom production of this scene you have been chosen to play the part of Demetrius or Helena.

How would you play your part? You might refer to tone of voice, movement, costume and facial expression.

Plan: **Helena**
- costume
- voice
- movement
- expression

I would choose to play the role of Helena. As this is a Shakespearean play I would presume that the costume is that of a period drama. Helena would wear a long corseted dress that is flowing to allow for movement, possibly in red to indicate her passionate nature. Her hair might be pinned up as was the fashion at the time, but because of her pleading it might be slightly unkempt.

I think Helena would be played as a strong-willed woman. She doesn't back down and pushes Demetrius to answer her. I think her tone of voice would vary. At times she is pleading with Demetrius and cajoling him. She flatters him to win his favour. Yet at other times she turns on him, 'you hard-hearted adamant'.

I think she would move around the stage to prevent Demetrius from leaving, perhaps even holding on to his leg when begging to be treated like his dog.

She tries to flirt with him throughout this piece so her facial expression would be playful at times, with lots of eye contact and smiling at him. She might try to look at him coyly from under her lashes and playfully punch him when she disagrees with him.

Q.3 Basing your answer on evidence from the text, would you like either Demetrius or Helena as a boyfriend or girlfriend? Support your answer by reference to the text.

Plan: **Boyfriend**
- rude
- insults
- coward
- lack of respect

I do not think that Demetrius would make a good boyfriend. He is rude and callous to Helena throughout the text. He bombards her with questions, 'Do I entice you? Do I speak you fair?' in order to make her stop. He tries to insult her at every opportunity, 'I am sick when I do look on thee'.

He almost threatens her when he warns her not to place herself 'into the hands of one who loves you not'.

He reveals his cowardice when he says 'I'll run from thee and hide me in the wood'. He would rather run away from her than deal with the situation. He then does threaten her when he says '*if thou do follow me, do not believe but I shall do thee mischief in the wood.*'

As he is a coward and a bully by threatening her when he does not get his own way, along with his rudeness and insulting behaviour I do not think I would like Demetrius as a boyfriend.

Sample question

The following extract (in edited form) is taken from *As You Like It* by William Shakespeare. Read the extract carefully and then answer the questions which follow.

> **Background to the extract:**
> * Rosalind is the daughter of the banished Duke Senior.
> * Celia is the daughter of Duke Frederick (Duke Senior's brother). Duke Frederick has taken over his brother's lands and now rules his Dukedom.
> * Rosalind and Celia are not only cousins but great friends.

Enter Duke Frederick with Lords.

Rosalind:	Look, here comes the Duke.
Celia:	With his eyes full of anger.
Duke Frederick:	Mistress, dispatch you with your safest haste,
	And get you from our Court.
Rosalind:	Me uncle?
Duke Frederick:	You cousin,
	Within these ten days if that thou be'st found
	So near our public Court as twenty miles,
	Thou diest for it.
Rosalind:	I do beseech your Grace,
	Let me the knowledge of my fault bear with me:
	Dear uncle,
	Never so much as in a thought unborn,
	Did I offend your Highness.
Duke Frederick:	Thus do all traitors,
	If their purgation[1] did consist in words,
	They are as innocent as grace itself;
	Let it suffice thee that I trust thee not.

[1]repentance

Rosalind:	Yet your mistrust cannot make me a traitor;
	Tell me whereon the likelihood depends.
Duke Frederick:	Thou art thy father's daughter, there's enough.
Rosalind:	So was I when your Highness took his Dukedom,
	So was I when your Highness banish'd him;
	My father was no traitor,
	Then good my Liege, mistake me not so much,
	To think my poverty is treacherous.
Celia:	Dear Sovereign hear me speak.
Duke Frederick:	Ay Celia, we stay'd her for your sake,
	Else had she with her father rang'd along.
Celia:	I did not then entreat to have her stay,
	It was your pleasure, and your own remorse;
	I was too young that time to value her,
	But now I know her: if she be a traitor,
	Why so am I: we still have stayed together,
	Rose at an instant, learn'd, play'd, eat together,
	And whereso'er we went, we went coupled and inseparable.
Duke Frederick:	She is too subtle for thee, and her smoothness,
	Her very silence, and her patience,
	Speak to the people, and they pity her:
	Thou art a fool, she robs thee of thy name,
	And thou wilt show more bright, and seem more virtuous
	When she is gone: then open not thy lips;
	Firm, and irrevocable is my doom,
	Which I have pass'd upon her, she is banish'd.
Celia:	Pronounce that sentence then on me my Liege,
	I cannot live out of her company.
Duke Frederick:	You are a fool: you niece prepare yourself,
	If you outstay the time, upon mine honour,
	And in the greatness of my word you die.

Exit Duke Frederick with Lords.

QUESTIONS

1. From your reading of this extract describe the character of Duke Frederick.
2. What kind of relationship is evident between Celia and Rosalind in this extract? Support your answer by reference to the text.

→

3. 'The Drama Continues'
   Write a scene that you imagine took place between Rosalind and Celia immediately after the above extract. Use appropriate dialogue and stage directions
   in answering.

   (Junior Certificate, 2003)

Other Drama

The following extract (in edited form) is taken from *Educating Rita* by Willy
Russell. Read the extract and then answer the questions which follow.

Background to the extract:
- As an adult learner, Rita is attending university to study literature.
- She is a housewife and also works as a hairdresser.
- She studies at home and comes to college on a regular basis to meet her
  literature tutor, Frank.

---

*Frank enters carrying a briefcase and a pile of essays. He takes sandwiches and an apple
from his briefcase and puts them on his desk and then goes to the window ledge and
dumps the essays and briefcase. He sits in a swivel chair, switches on the radio, opens
the packet of sandwiches, takes a bite and then picks up a book and starts reading.*

Rita bursts through the door out of breath.

Frank: What are you doing here? *(He looks at his watch)* It's Thursday, you . . .
Rita: *(moving over to the desk quickly)* I know I shouldn't be here, it's me dinner
             hour, but listen, I've gorra tell someone, have y' got a few minutes, can y'
             spare . . . ?
Frank: *(alarmed)* My God, what is it?
Rita: I had to come an' tell y', Frank, last night, I went to the theatre! A proper
             one, a professional theatre.
             Frank gets up and switches off the radio and then returns to the swivel chair
Frank: *(sighing)* For God's sake, you had me worried, I thought it was something
             serious.
Rita: No, listen, it was. I went out an' got me ticket, it was Shakespeare, I thought
             it was gonna be dead borin' . . .
Frank: Then why did you go in the first place?

Rita: I wanted to find out. But listen, it wasn't borin', it was bleedin' great, honest, ogh, it done me in, it was fantastic. I'm gonna do an essay on it.

Frank: *(smiling)* Come on, which one was it?

Rita moves right up centre

Rita: ' . . . Out, out, brief candle!
Life's but a walking shadow, a poor player
That struts and frets his hour upon the stage
And then is heard no more. It is a tale
Told by an idiot, full of sound and fury
Signifying nothing.'

Frank: *(deliberately)* Ah, 'Romeo and Juliet'.

Rita: *(moving towards Frank)* Tch. Frank! Be serious. I learnt that today from the book. *(She produces a copy of 'Macbeth')* Look, I went out an' bought the book. Isn't it great? What I couldn't get over is how excitin' it was.

Frank puts his feet up on the desk.

Rita: Wasn't his wife a cow, eh? An' that fantastic bit where he meets Macduff an' he thinks he's all invincible. I was on the edge of me seat at that bit. I wanted to shout out an' tell Macbeth, warn him.

Frank: You didn't, did you?

Rita: Nah. Y' can't do that in a theatre, can y'? It was dead good. It was like a thriller.

Frank: Yes. You'll have to go and see more.

Rita: I'm goin' to. *Macbeth's* a tragedy, isn't it?

Frank nods

Rita: Right. *(She smiles at Frank and he smiles back at her)* Well I just – I just had to tell someone who'd understand.

Frank: I'm honoured that you chose me.

Rita: *(moving towards the door)* Well, I better get back. I've left a customer with a perm lotion. If I don't get a move on there'll be another tragedy.

QUESTIONS

1. You are presented with the opportunity of ending up on a desert island with one of these two characters. Which one would you choose and why?
2. Do you think Rita is a good student? Give reasons for your answer based on evidence from the text.
3. For a classroom production of this scene you have been chosen to play the part of Frank or Rita. How would you play your part? You might refer to tone of voice, movement, costume and facial expression. *(Junior Certificate, 2002)*

SAMPLE ANSWERS

Only *two* of the following answers are necessary.

Q1. You are presented with the opportunity of ending up on a desert island with one of these two characters. Which one would you chose and why?

Plan: **Frank**
- laid back
- sense of humour
- sincere
- positive
- interesting

I would chose Frank as he seems to be very laid back, nothing seems to faze him. He remains cool throughout the scene despite Rita's high energy.

He is very knowledgeable. His knowledge of literature and theatre would pass away the time on a desert island.

He makes light of Rita's quotation by pretending it was from Romeo and Juliet so he obviously has a sense of humour. He is very encouraging as he says, '*You'll have to go and see more*'.

He seems very sincere when he replies to her statement that he was the only one who would understand, '*I'm honoured that you chose me*'.

Even though he has been interrupted he gives Rita the time to talk. He doesn't respond negatively to the intrusion. He questions her on her experience, '*Come on, which one was it?*' and seems genuinely interested in her opinions.

As he is sincere, interesting, relaxed and genuine, he is the one I would like to end up on a desert island with.

Q2. Do you think Rita is a good student? Give reasons for your answer based on evidence from the text.

Plan: **Rita**
- enthusiastic
- good memory
- serious
- involved
- scattered

I think Rita is a very enthusiastic student. She is committed to her studies. She went to see a Shakespearean play even though she 'thought it was gonna be dead borin''.

She is enthusiastic in her response to the play, 'it wasn't borin', it was bleedin' great, honest'. Even though this was something she didn't have to do she wanted to experience the theatre.

She seems to have a good memory as she quotes six lines from Macbeth easily, 'Out, out, brief candle . . .'. She followed up the experience by going out and buying the book. This shows the extent of her seriousness about her studies. She has remembered key points of the play, 'That fantastic bit where he meets Macduff', and was fully involved in the experience, 'I was on the edge of my seat at that bit'.

However she also seems quite distracted and scatty. She has to leave because she 'left a customer with a perm lotion'. Rita is probably quite a good student if a little unorthodox.

Q.3 For a classroom production of this scene you have been chosen to play the part of Frank or Rita.

How would you play the part? You might refer to tone of voice, movement, costume and facial expression.

Plan: **Rita**
- animated movement
- costume
- voice, colloquial, accent
- expression

In this scene I would chose to play Rita. I think she would be very animated in this scene and full of life. As she is on a lunch break from a hair salon she may be wearing an apron of some sort over her clothes. She is a housewife also, so she would not be very glamorous. However the impression of Rita from the extract is of a very brash, loud person. Her costume therefore may be simple like a pair of jeans with a brightly coloured shirt covered with a salon-like apron. She would also wear big earrings and have bright red painted nails and be heavily made-up.

Throughout the script she moves around the room, so her movements would be very energetic and spontaneous.

In the extract she seems to have an accent, 'I gorra tell someone'. The script uses a lots of colloquialisms where the final letters are dropped from words, 'can y' spare?' 'borin' 'bleedin'. So to play Rita I would have to adopt a similar accent.

However when she is quoting from Shakespeare her accent changes and she has perfect diction. As with everything else about Rita her facial expressions would be exaggerated and over the top. She probably makes a lot of hand gestures as she seems very demonstrative.

I think Rita would be played as a slightly scatty character. Her enthusiasm and energy dominate the scene, which contrast with the stillness of Frank.

SAMPLE QUESTION

The following extract (in edited form) is taken from *The Crazy Wall* by JB Keane. Read the extract carefully and answer the questions which follow.

Background to the extract:
- Lelum is the son of Mary and Michael.
- They live in Ireland in the 1940s.
- As this extract begins Michael is gone to the river to collect more gravel for the wall he is building.

Lelum: If he doesn't come back soon this stuff will be gone hard. Where did he go anyway?

Mary: To the river for more gravel.

Lelum: What a wall this is going to be.

Mary: Come here Lelum and hold this yank of wool for me.
(He sits on the seat and extends his hands. She entwines the wool round them and starts to make a ball of thread)

Lelum: I think he is using the wall to avoid reality.

Mary: I suppose in a way you're right but we're all the same aren't we? We all need something to hide behind at times. You and he don't seem to be hitting it off lately. I think you're under the impression he's failed you.

Lelum: Well hasn't he?

Mary: You mean because he didn't send you to university?

Lelum: Among other things.

Mary: If you were an only son Lelum or if there were only two or even three of you the university would be no problem but there are four of you then there are the girls. You don't know how lucky you are to have received a secondary education. When I was a girl only one in a hundred was so lucky.

Lelum: If he didn't drink so much.

Mary: He's never refused me anything. We don't know what hunger is. We have a fine home.

Lelum:	I don't know what to do. I've no job.
Mary:	You have your job in the fields.
Lelum:	We both know there's no future there. Anyway there's only another month of it.
Mary:	You'll get a job and what's more you'll get a good job. You have brains Lelum and you're a good worker. You're young and strong and you're good looking. It's only a matter of time.
Lelum:	I know what I'd really like to do but I'm almost afraid to say it.
Mary:	You can say it to me. That's as far as 'twill go. Come on Lelum. You and I are too fond of each other to have secrets.
Lelum:	Well . . . I'd like to become a professional actor . . . aren't you going to laugh?
Mary:	Why would I laugh?
Lelum:	Nobody from this town ever became a professional actor.
Mary:	I should think that would be a reflection on the town.
Lelum:	You mean you'd approve?
Mary:	If it's what you really want Lelum I approve. I'll do all in my power to help you. Have you done anything about it?
Lelum:	I spoke to Mr McMaster the last time he was here and he promised me an audition this time round. They'll be in town next week.
Mary:	What will the audition consist of?
Lelum:	A piece of my own choice from Shakespeare. I've ordered a copy of *Romeo and Juliet* from a bookshop in Dublin. I'll do the balcony scene.
Mary:	That would be marvellous.
Lelum:	What about himself?
Mary:	You picked an unfortunate profession. He hates actors.
Lelum:	I know. I've heard him.
Mary:	According to him they're all idlers.
Lelum:	Better say nothing then.
Mary:	Not for the present. You go ahead with your plans. We'll work it out. You know . . . I think you'd make a marvellous actor. There's something about you. I acted in a play once, *The Colleen Bawn*.
Lelum:	I think the gravel-seekers are back.
Mary:	Not a word about acting.

QUESTIONS

1. What kind of relationship is evident between Lelum and his mother? Support your answer by reference to the extract.
2. Describe the kind of person you expect Lelum's father to be. In your answer you should refer to his father's *appearance* and *personality*.

→

3. 'The Drama Continues'

Write the scene that you imagine took place between Lelum and his father when Lelum told him of his wish to be an actor. Use appropriate dialogue and stage directions in answering. *(Junior Certificate, 2003)*

Studied Drama

SAMPLE QUESTIONS

Attempt the following questions:

1. Select a play you have studied.

Give an account of a dramatic scene or part of the play.

How was the drama created?

Base your answer on the text studied. If you wish you may also make reference to a theatre performance or a film version you have seen of the play.

2. Plays deal with many interesting themes.

Select a play you have studied.

Outline a theme in it you found interesting.

Would you consider the theme to be relevant to your own life and/or to the world around you? Explain your answer with reference to the play.

(Junior Certificate, 2002)

1. Choose a relationship from a play you have studied.
   (a) Outline how this relationship develops throughout the play.   (15)
   (b) Which of the characters in the relationship made most impact on you? Give reasons for your answer making reference to the play.   (15)
2. Select a play you have studied.
   (a) What did you learn about the world the characters of the play lived in? Support your answer by reference to the play   (20)
   (b) Did you like or dislike this world? Give reasons for your answer making reference to the play.   (10)

(Junior Certificate, 2003)

SAMPLE ANSWER ON STUDIED DRAMA

Q.2 (2003)
(a) What did you learn about the world the characters of the play lived in?

In the play *The Merchant of Venice* by William Shakespeare, the world that is described is very different to today. This can be seen in the way characters are treated and what is expected of them. But some things like love and money remain the same.

Antonio is sad at the beginning of the play. The others on stage presume money problems are his cause of concern, '*had I such venture forth, the better part of my affections would be with my hopes abroad.*' Antonio's monetary problems lead to his bond with Shylock. This, like a modern stock market crash, leaves those in debt to seek desperate means of securing their survival. Antonio promises to repay Shylock with a pound of his flesh if his finances don't improve. This extreme is not present in today's world but the desperation is the same.

Then, as now, the course of true love never does run smooth. The sub-plot involving Jessica and Lorenzo and the trifling matter of Portia's ring shows us that in their world there are many things that may impede the course of true love. In their world the disapproval of a father was a serious matter to be overcome.

We know that women were not treated well in this society. Portia, even though she is rich, is subject to the conditions of her father's will. She must accept the suitor that correctly chooses a casket. She has no choice in the matter, '*I may neither choose who I would nor refuse who I dislike.*' In addition to this, Portia's position is further undermined by the fact that women were not given positions of power or authority. In order to convince the court to listen to her, Portia must disguise herself as a man. She proves that she is more intelligent than the men around her by working out the flaw in Shylock's plan and saving Antonio, a feat that none of the men present could do.

The power of the law is important in the world of the characters. Even though it seems to be unfair to Antonio, the Duke has no recourse but to uphold the law. If it wasn't for Portia's intervention Shylock would have received his pound of flesh and Antonio would have died.

In the world of the characters, as with our world, racism and prejudice were common. In this case particularly, religious difference is the cause of distrust. This sectarianism is still present in our world but the *Merchant of Venice* proves it is not a modern phenomenon. Shylock says of Antonio '*I hate him for he is a Christian,*' but he also tells us of the abuse he has endured, '*You call me misbeliever, cut-throat dog and spit upon my Jewish gabardine.*'

(b) Did you like or dislike this world?

I would not like to live in this world as it seems barbarous and cruel. A court that would accept the cruel torture of Antonio as a reasonable course of action is not one I would like to be subject to.

As Shylock says '*The court awards it, and the law doth give it*'. If Portia hadn't stopped Shylock from shedding '*one drop of Christian blood*' Antonio would have died.

A world where a woman must marry a person who correctly guesses the contents of a casket is also not one I would like to inhabit. It seems a very foolish way of deciding your fate. The fact that Portia had to disguise herself as a man in order to be taken seriously is also a negative point for this world.

Unfortunately a lot of the vices that are described in the world of The Merchant of Venice are still present in today's world. Prejudice and racism are still with us. The anti-Semitism displayed by Bassanio and Antonio is not as openly accepted in today's world. Antonio does not repent his remarks, '*I am as like to call thee so again.*'

Overall, I do not like the world that is presented to us in *The Merchant of Venice.*

6
Poetry

UNDERSTANDING POETRY

Poets try to capture a moment, event, emotion or character in words. Unlike a story, a poem focuses on the heart of the matter. *Every* word has significance. Poets choose certain words because they help to convey a particular mood or tone. Poets use certain techniques to convey their meaning and a grasp of these techniques will ensure a greater understanding and appreciation of the poem. Poetry can deal with many different themes in varying ways. Some poets may use humour or satire to deal with a serious topic, or conversely a poet may deal with a light-hearted subject in a serious manner. The tone used is a good indicator for how the poet wishes the theme to be treated.

The Exam Paper

The poetry section is divided into two main parts: the unseen poetry and the studied poetry. You have to answer both sections.

THE UNSEEN POETRY

In the unseen section a poem is printed on the paper and questions asked regarding your understanding of the poem. There are thirty marks for this section. Typical questions asked are:

- What imagery is used in the poem?
- What type of person do you think the poet is?
- Did you like or dislike the poem?
- What was the main point of the poem?
- Comment on the language/rhythm/style used.
- Comment on the mood of the poem.

- Who is speaking in the poem?
- To whom is the poem addressed?

Exam hints

- It is essential that you read the poem several times before answering the questions to ensure you understand the poem fully. Read any explanations at the start as they may reveal more about the subject matter of the poem. After reading the poem the first time, read the questions as they may provide you with further insights into the poem or the poet's intentions. Re-read the poem again before answering.
- While the questions often ask for your opinions on the poetry try not to be overwhelmingly negative. A balanced answer well supported by relevant quotation will gain far more marks than a one-line answer stating you disliked the poem.
- Use quotations to support any points you make. This shows that you have read the poem and can identify the relevant parts of it for your answer. The quotations you use should not be very long, as this just looks like you are trying to fill up your answer, but a short relevant quote shows you are aware of the pertinent points.
- Frame your answers with a point and a quotation in each paragraph.
- Don't over write on this section. Look at the marks awarded for each question and frame your answers accordingly.

THE STUDIED POETRY

In this section you will be asked to answer on poetry that you have studied in class. There are thirty marks for this section. The questions are very general to allow you to answer on a poem or poems of your choice.

In recent years the types of questions asked were:

- Poetry celebrates a person/place/thing. Discuss.
- What poet did you like best? Why? – WB Yeats
- Compare two poems with a similar theme.
- Discuss a poem that made you think. Discuss the type of language used.
- Discuss the poem you liked best and least. Give explanations.
- Write an introduction for a poem you liked explaining why it should be included in an anthology of poetry.
- Discuss a poem that is written in an unusual style.
- Discuss a poem that deals with behaviour or an issue in society.

- What is good poetry? Discuss in relation to the poetry you have studied.
- Discuss a poem that creates a certain mood/atmosphere. How is it created?
- You may also be asked to write about a poem that deals with a particular theme such as: childhood, relationships, memories, war, school, nature and love.

Exam hints

- Make sure you have an adequate selection of poetry to choose from for your answer. You should have studied poetry that deals with varying themes such as childhood, nature, memories, relationships and war. You may be asked to discuss two poems that deal with a similar theme so you should have this covered.
- Form opinions about the poetry you have studied. You may be asked why you choose them so be prepared. Reasons why you liked a particular poem may be:
  - Because the theme appealed to you.
  - Because the poet speaks with sincerity that resonates with you, the reader.
  - Because his use of imagery appealed to your senses.
  - Because you liked his use of language, tone, atmosphere or rhythm.
- Quote from the poem to support any point you make. The quotations don't have to be long but they do need to be relevant.
- You should have prepared work on an individual poet. Two or three poems by this poet will suffice. Look at the different themes tackled by the poet and how they are handled differently in each poem. Also look for similarities in the work. Does the poet use a certain style, type of language, rhythm pattern or imagery?

Key points to look out for

- **Theme**

The theme is what the poem is about, the central message of the poem. Some poets may take a simple theme such as love but give varying opinions on it throughout the poem. Sample themes: love, war, childhood, memories and relationships.

- **Tone**

Tone relates to the tone of voice the poet would use if the poem were read aloud. How would the poet say certain lines in the poem? Is the narrator angry, passionate, depressed, reminiscing or disappointed? Does this tone vary in the poem? Is there a development of the poet's thought throughout the poem?

• Mood

Mood relates to the emotion or emotions felt by the poet/narrator throughout the poem. What is the mood of the speaker in the poem? Is it happy, sad, nostalgic or frustrated? Are there images or words that convey this mood effectively?

• Imagery

Essentially imagery means the pictures created in the mind of the reader by the words of the poet. What descriptions does the poet give of his/her experience? Are there any unusual images? Does the poet place contrasting images together? What effect does this have?

To create images poets often use some poetic devices. It may help your understanding of poetry to identify some of these key devices.

Simile:	A comparison using the words like or as, e.g. 'Coughing *like* hags'.
Metaphor:	A comparison not using the words like or as, e.g. 'Our cries are wolves howling'.
Alliteration:	When words that begin with the same letter are placed in close proximity to each other, e.g. 'Forest's ferny floor'
Assonance:	When vowel (a, e, i, o, u) sounds are repeated, e.g. 'Moonlit door'.

Other features of poetry on which you may be asked to comment are rhythm and language.

• Rhythm

How does the poet create a sense of rhythm in the poem? Does the rhyming scheme make the poem seem simple and fast paced? Does the use of assonance slow down certain lines? What effect does that have on the rest of the poem? Do short clipped words give a staccato effect?

• Language

Does the poet use simple language that is easily understood? Are some words used that are obviously common only in a certain place (colloquialism)? Does the poet use slang words or words that are common only in a certain generation? How does the poet's choice of words affect the tone of the poem?

Examination Questions: The Unseen Poem

Read the poem and then answer the questions which follow.

Poem for Lara, 10

An ashtree on fire,
the hair of your head
coaxing larks
with your sweet voice
in the green grass,
a crowd of daisies
playing with you,
a crowd of rabbits
dancing with you,
the blackbird
with its gold bill
is a jewel for you,
the goldfinch
with its sweetness
is your music.
You are perfume,
you are honey,
a wild strawberry:
even the bees think you
a flower in the field.
Little queen in the land of books,
may you be always thus,
may you ever be free
from sorrow-chains.

Here's my blessing for you, girl,
it is no petty grace –
may you have your mother's soul
and the beauty of her face.

Michael Hartnett

QUESTIONS

Answer **two** of the following questions.

1. From the imagery the poet uses, what impression of Lara do you get?

2. From your reading of the poem, what type of person do you think Michael Hartnett was?

3. Did you like or dislike the poem? Give reasons for your answer based on evidence from the poem.

(Junior Certificate, 2002)

SAMPLE ANSWER

*Only **two** of the following are necessary. For a fifteen-mark question you should make at least three points supported by quotations.*

1. The poet uses a wide variety of images to portray his daughter Lara. He begins with a physical description, '*An ashtree on fire, the hair of your head*'. This gives us the impression that she has red hair but also that she is vibrant and full of life.

   Throughout the poem Lara is associated with sweetness and melody, '*your sweet voice*' and '*its sweetness is your music*'. Like a fairytale character she is depicted as playing with wild animals, '*a crowd of rabbits dancing with you*', and she seems at one with the nature around her.

   The poet uses the sensual images of '*perfume*', '*wild strawberry*' and '*honey*' and this creates the impression that Lara is sweet, pure and innocent and full of innate goodness.

2. Michael Hartnett obviously loves his daughter. He has idealised his vision of her playing in the fields. She has become so assimilated into the landscape that the bees think of her as '*a flower in the fields*'. But while he is depicting her as carefree, he is realistic and aware that such innocence and purity are threatened in the modern world. He wishes that she will remain '*free from sorrow-chains*'.

   He also shows great affection for his wife. His greatest wish for his daughter is not for wealth or success but for her to have her '*mother's soul and the beauty of her face*'.

3. I liked the poem because it gave a very vivid depiction of the youthful exuberance of a young girl. She is described as '*coaxing*', '*playing*' and '*dancing*' and gives the impression of having boundless energy.

   I also liked the images used in the poem. The image of a '*little queen of the land of books*' is reminiscent of many fairytale characters like Alice in Wonderland. Lara is in her own little world where she reigns supreme and her subjects, the larks, rabbits and blackbird, all dance in attendance.

Finally I particularly like the final stanza of the poem. Like other fairytales where wishes are bestowed on little princesses, here the poet wishes that his daughter has her '*mother's soul and the beauty of her face*'. The poet gives his daughter what he considers to be the most important blessing and this brings some of the fairytale qualities into reality.

Read the following poem by Gareth Owen and then answer the questions which follow.

Space Shot

Out of the furnace
The great fish rose
Its silver tail on fire
But with a slowness
Like something sorry
To be rid of earth.
The boiling mountains
Of snow white cloud
Searched for a space to go into
And the ground thundered
With a roar
That set teacups
Rattling in the kitchen
Twenty miles away.
Across the blue it arched
Milk bottle white
But shimmering in the haze.
And the watchers by the fence
Held tinted glass against their eyes
And wondered at what man could do
To make so large a thing
To fly so far and free
While the unknown Universe waited;
For waiting
Was what it had always been good at.

Gareth Owen

QUESTIONS

Attempt the following questions:

1. You are one of 'the watchers by the fence' looking at this spectacle. Describe, in your own words, what you see and outline your thoughts and feelings at the time.
2. Do you think Gareth Owen is a poet you would like to read more of? Based on the evidence from this poem give reasons for your answer.

(Junior Certificate, 2003)

Examination Question: Studied Poetry

Answer either 1 or 2 which follow. (30 marks)

1. *Michael Hartnett once said that poetry gave him the power to love and celebrate.*
   - Select a poem you have studied which celebrates a person, place or thing.
   - Give a brief outline of the theme of the poem.
   - How is the sense of celebration created?

OR

2. From the poetry you have studied choose the poet you liked best of all. Explain why you liked this poet's work and support your answer by reference to his/her poetry.

(Junior Certificate, 2002)

SAMPLE ANSWER

Be sure when answering that you address all the terms of the question.

> **Answer to point one**

1. The poem that I feel celebrates a place is 'To Daffodils' by William Wordsworth.

   In this poem the poet describes a walk he took where he came upon a field of daffodils. The sight of the flowers filled the poet with joy and he describes the scene in detail. In the final stanza the poet says that the memory of that sight has filled him with joy on occasions when he has been alone and thoughtful. The theme of the poem is the beauty of nature and how it can bring pleasure to the observer.

> **Answer to point two**

   The sense of celebration is created in the poem through the poet's use of imagery and vibrant language. He begins by describing himself as a cloud *'that floats on high o'er vales and hills'*. This simile describes his aimless wandering that is interrupted by the sight of the daffodils. The words '*golden*' and '*dancing*' help to create a sense of celebration. The daffodils seem to take on human characteristics and be filled with the joy of being alive. Their lively dance makes such an impression on the poet that he is compelled to write about them.

In the second stanza the poet continues his description of the scene by comparing the daffodils to the waves on the shoreline. Again the celebration of the beauty and vivaciousness of the daffodils is portrayed in the comparison, '*they outdid the sparkling waves with glee*'. They have almost hypnotised the poet as he '*gazed and gazed but little thought*'. He is totally captivated by the scene. Their performance is viewed as a '*show*', purely for the benefit of the poet. As he ponders their dance he says that the sight has brought him wealth, but the word '*wealth*' in this case is not associated with monetary value but with the spiritual value the poet places on the vision.

> Answer to point three

In the final stanza the poet leaves the scene, but he still celebrates the vision by reflecting on it in moments of solitude. The imagination is referred to as '*that inward eye*' and it is here that the vision of the daffodils remains. His use of words such as '*bliss*' and '*pleasure*' help to capture his sense of joy at even the remembrance of the sight.

The final two lines of the poem capture the sense of joy and celebration that the poet has experienced when looking at the daffodils. '*Then my heart with pleasure fills and dances with the daffodils*'. This to me is the high point of the poem as the poet can now join the daffodils in their joyful dance. Through the power of the imagination the poet is free to celebrate life.

OR

> Reasons for liking his poetry

2. From the poetry I have studied, the poet whose work I liked best was Seamus Heaney.

I enjoyed his work because he deals with a variety of <u>themes</u> such as nature, memories and childhood, but throughout all his work there is a sense of his <u>personal experience</u>. This gives a level of sincerity to the poetry that makes it appealing. He also uses very <u>vivid imagery</u> to portray scene and to draw the reader into the poem.

> Reasons with support

In his poem 'Mid-Term Break', Heaney describes a very <u>personal experience</u>: the death of his younger brother. He writes the poem from the perspective of a young boy who is still in shock and doesn't quite understand the enormity of the situation. As he sits in the school sickbay Heaney uses <u>alliteration</u> to describe the ominous ringing of the bells '*knelling classes to a close*'.

Reasons
with
support

Heaney describes the scene at the house very accurately. The platitudes of the neighbours, '*it was a hard blow*' and the incongruous laughing of the baby, '*the baby cooed and laughed and rocked the pram*' aptly describe the scene.

I particularly liked the way Heaney used <u>adjectives</u> to capture the frustration of his mother, '*angry tearless sighs*', at the injustice of the situation.

Like any young boy, the reality of death doesn't hit the poet until he sees the body, until then his brother is referred to as '*the corpse*'. I liked the way the poet created the <u>tender image</u> of the bedside. The image of '*snowdrops and candles*' soothing the bedside are in total contrast with the underlying tension of the previous stanzas.

The most powerful image in the poem is of the '*four foot box*'. His brother lies there '*as in his cot*' emphasising how young and babyish his brother was. Heaney repeats the line adding '*a foot for every year*'. This makes the scene very poignant and the sense of loss and injustice of this death is well captured by Heaney in that very simple line.

In contrast to this poem, 'Early Purges' also deals with death but this time Heaney explores the necessity for death as part of nature. I found that the <u>imagery</u> used in this poem was also very vivid but unlike 'Mid-term Break' Heaney doesn't shy away from death but instead he describes in-depth the details of the kittens' drowning, '*soft paws scraping like mad*', '*the three sogged remains turn mealy and crisp*'. Again he writes from the perspective of a young boy who has to face his fears and this adds to the sense of sincerity that makes the poem so appealing.

By the end of the poem the boy has grown up and learns to deal with and accept the necessary deaths on the farm '*on well run farms pests have to be kept down*'.

Overall, the poetry of Heaney appealed to me because of the evident sincerity of the lines and the vivid nature of his depictions of the scenes of his childhood.

SAMPLE QUESTIONS FOR STUDIED POETRY

(Junior Certificate, 2003)
1. '*Poetry can tell us what human beings are*' Maya Angelou
    (a) Select a poem you have studied which deals with a human being. Outline the picture you get of this person from the poem.
    (b) How has the poet created this picture? Support your answer by reference to or quotation from the poem you have studied.

OR

2. Select a poem where the imagery is very powerful.
    (a) What for you was the message of this poem?
    (b) Describe how the imagery helped to develop this message. Support your
        answer by reference to or quotation from the poem you have studied.

(Junior Certificate, 2001)
1. Choose two poems which deal with a similar theme. Name the poems,
    poet(s) and theme dealt with and discuss how each poem deals with the
    theme.
2. Which poem did you prefer and why?

(Junior Certificate, 2000)
1. From the poetry you have studied choose one poem to which the two
    following comments apply:
    – The poem made me think.
    – I liked the language in the poem.
Explain how these comments apply to the poem you have chosen.

OR

2. Name the poem studied by you, that you like best, and the poem studied by
    you that you like least. Explain, by comparing the two, why you liked the one
    and disliked the other.

7
Fiction

As with the other sections on Paper 2 the Fiction section is allocated sixty marks – thirty for answers based on an unseen extract and thirty marks for your answers on the novel or short story studied by you.

Unseen Fiction

There are two types of question asked on the unseen extract; those based on comprehension of the extract and those based on your analysis of the style of writing. Close reading of the extract is required. Although this may seem similar to the Reading section on Paper 1 this section requires you to use your knowledge of fiction writing and awareness of writing style to answer the question.

COMPREHENSION QUESTIONS

The most frequently asked question is: 'What type of character is xx in the extract?'

In your answer you should examine the extract carefully to find quotations to support any assertions you make. Divide your answer into paragraphs, giving a key word and at least one supporting reference in each. For a fifteen-mark question you should have at least three paragraphs.

Key word

SAMPLE ANSWER

In this extract Mary is obviously a very passionate person. We see this when she . . . and in her outburst where she states ' . . . .'

Reference and quote

The amount of character traits you may recognise is endless but here are a few you may frequently find.

Characteristics

Bossy, bully, laid-back, relaxed, humorous, glamorous, staid, boring, weak, coward, brave, courageous, emotional, pathetic, passionate, enthusiastic, inspirational, ruthless, tyrant, naïve, innocent, honest, sycophant (licks up to), superficial, powerful, biased.

Other comprehension questions include:

*   The setting
*   The relationship between characters
*   Comparisons between attitudes evident.

CRITICAL ANALYSIS

You will be asked questions that require you to examine the work of the author in a critical fashion. (Remembering that to be critical does not mean to be negative but instead to examine carefully and objectively.) The following may help you structure your answer.

1. Storyline/plot

Is the plot believable? Does the author create tension and suspense? Is the writer very factual and clinical? Is it an autobiography? Is it told in the first person, (i.e. 'I')? Is it subjective? Or can the author distance himself and be objective?

Is there a logical structure? Does the piece flow? Does the extract develop the storyline/characters?

2. Characters

Are the characters well described? How do they speak? How do they act? Are there any obvious contrasts apparent? What adjectives does the writer use to describe the main characters?

3. Style

How is the piece written?
*   Is there a lot of dialogue? Does this give the piece a sense of immediacy?
*   Is there a lot of description of place, character or mood? What kind of atmosphere does this create? Does this create tension or suspense?

- Does the writer use colloquialisms (informal language or sayings/patterns of speech found in a locality)? Does this make the piece more authentic, more real or more dramatic?
- Does the writer use poetic devices such as metaphors, similes, alliteration, assonance or repetition?
- Does the writer use a lot of lists to give a sense of place or to develop a character? Is there a lot of factual information?
- Does the writer use literary references or biblical references to support his/her point of view? Does this give the impression that the writer is well educated?
- Look at the sentence structure/syntax of the piece. Does the writer use varying sentence lengths in the extract? Are there long detailed sentences followed by short snappy sentences?
- Does the writer use rhetorical questions in the extract?

Hint
Use these headings to answer a question on whether you liked the piece or not. Try not to be overly negative when answering this type of question. By answering positively you allow yourself far more scope to write about the piece and so gain marks.

Studied Fiction

Similar headings also apply to the novel or selection of short stories you have studied. In the novel/short story you intend to write about for your exam, you should know about each of the following in detail.

1. **Plot**
   What happens? To whom? When?
   - You should know in detail and be able to write about key scenes such as scenes of conflict, or resolution or of dramatic tension.
   - What lead up to these scenes?
   - What happened?
   - How was it resolved?
   - What effects did this have on the characters or the plot?

2. **Characters**
   You should know each of the main characters in detail.

- Be able to outline their importance in the plot.
- What type of person are they? What do we know about them? How are they described by the author? What do they do? What do they say?
- Be able to give examples of each of their character traits in the novel/short story. Quotation or reference to events in the story are sufficient support for your answer.
- How have they influenced other characters? Have they been a positive or negative influence? Why?

3. Setting

The novel/short story you have studied is set in a particular time and place that you should be familiar with.

- Can you accurately describe the setting in the novel you have studied?
- How is it different to your own experience?
- Does the time/setting influence the events in the novel?
- Have attitudes changed?

4. Themes/Issues

A range of themes or issues may be dealt with in any text. You should be able to discuss the theme/s dealt with in the novel you have studied.

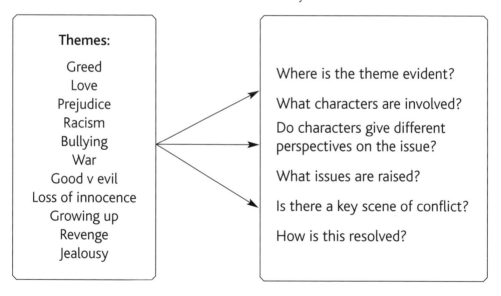

Themes:

Greed
Love
Prejudice
Racism
Bullying
War
Good v evil
Loss of innocence
Growing up
Revenge
Jealousy

Where is the theme evident?

What characters are involved?

Do characters give different perspectives on the issue?

What issues are raised?

Is there a key scene of conflict?

How is this resolved?

5. Style

As with the unseen fiction you should be aware of aspects of style as outlined above. In addition the type of novel/short story you are dealing with influences the style in which it is written.

- Most novels/short stories are written as *third person narratives*. That is, they tell the story as if the writer is external to events. (He did . . . She went . . .)
- An *autobiography*, however, tells the story purely from one person's point of view – the author's. This type of novel can be biased as only one side of the story is told. But as it is based on real life events it is not a fictional story.
- A fictional novel may be told from one person's point of view. This is a *first person narrative*. An example of this type of novel is *The Diary of Adrian Mole*. All events in this novel are told from his point of view as the novel is written in *diary format*.
- Look at the structure of the novel you have studied. Does one event follow another (*linear format*)? Or does the author use *flashbacks* to fill us in on details of past events?
- A novel such as *To Kill a Mockingbird* is told entirely through flashback. The narrator (the person telling us the story) tells us that these events took place when she was a child. This technique gives us a *dual perspective* on these events i.e. the adult looking back and the child's view of them at the time.
- A *biography* is a non-fictional account of a person's life. As it is based on more than one source of information it tends to be less biased than an autobiography. But, as it is not written by someone directly involved, it is based on hearsay and not the inner thoughts of the central character.

Look at the novel you have studied and identify the key elements of how the story is told.

QUESTIONS

1. Outline the plot of the novel you have studied in your own words.
2. Choose a character who made a significant impact on another person's life.
   - Outline this character's influence supporting your answer with reference.
   - Would you like to encounter this person in your own life? Give reasons for your answer.

(Junior Certificate, 2002)

3. 'A good novel/short story holds your attention from beginning to end.'
   To what extent is this true of any novel/short story studied by you? You may wish to refer to the storyline, the characters, the style of writing, the author's holding back information until late in the novel or short story.

(Junior Certificate, 2001)

4. Select a novel or short story you have studied that deals with conflict or difficulties. Explain:
   - How this conflict or these difficulties arose.
   - To what extent the conflict or difficulty was resolved.
     Support your answer by reference to the novel or short story.

(Junior Certificate, 2002)

SAMPLE ANSWERS

Read carefully the following extract and then answer the questions. The extract (in edited form) is taken from 'Miss McDwyer', a short story, by Cathy Toft.

Background to the text:
This extract deals with the experiences of an English teacher, Miss McDwyer, who substitutes for Mr Hennessy, the regular teacher.

Miss McDwyer

'Is this Mr Hennessy's English class?' she asked timidly. Her voice was very low. Almost a whisper.

'Yes,' chorused a few voices.

She closed the door. I looked up and held my breath.

'I am Miss McDwyer. I will be teaching here for a while.'

I glanced outside. It had stopped raining.

'This is my first year teaching,' her quiet voice told us as she smiled across the room.

That was her first fatal mistake. Even as she said it I saw the boys' deadpan eyes brighten. Their set mouths curved into smiles. She spoke of the course, of the books we would study, of the things we would do. I was interested. To my utmost surprise, I was interested in English.

'We will begin tomorrow,' she said. 'We have a lot to get through.'

Sometimes when she spoke she stumbled on her words. Self-consciously she kept tucking a curl behind her ear. The boys' eyes sparkled wickedly. They were like tigers watching their prey. Soon they would move in for the kill.

We started the next day. Miss McDwyer was early for class. She was full of enthusiasm. So much so, we thought she would burst.

'We will start with a short story.' There was a lot of moaning and groaning. 'It's called "Old House" and is written by James Brown.'

There was uproar. James Brown must be the most boring, dull writer in the history of mankind. Even his name was boring.

She beamed. 'You will be surprised what you will find in a short story.'

Laughter filled the room. What could possibly be found in a short story?

She was right. We were surprised. There were hidden meanings behind the words, secret messages buried within masked symbols, found only after much uncovering. It was almost as if we were lost in a maze and trying to work our way out. I was so absorbed in my work I did not hear the bell dong drearily throughout the school. Already I was looking forward to the next class.

We started another short story. 'This is called "The Windows of Wonder" and was written by Bryan McMahon,' she informed us. 'Now you can really see the art of the short story.'

I set about it with zest. Nothing was ordinary any more. Everything glinted and shimmered. The words were no longer black and white. They were yellow and purple and red, wavering and contracting, pacing and dancing. Something ignited in me.

She introduced Library. I soon found myself in fascinating new worlds which seized me from my normal lifestyle, clasped my imagination, clutched my mind. It was my release. She opened up a whole new world for me. She caught my attention immediately and it never wavered. My head was filled with amazing thoughts which flowed onto paper, complicated stories suddenly became clear. I was a different person.

My classmates were not as easy a conquest. They were in permanent shadow. Her ideas fell on deaf ears, her world of colour remained for them a world of darkness.

After one week the paper fights began.

From 'Miss McDwyer' by Cathy Toft

Questions

Answer **two** of the following. Each question is worth fifteen marks.

1. What kind of teacher do you think Miss McDwyer is? Give reasons for your answer.
2. This short story was a winning entry in an under-16 national writing competition. Basing your evidence on the above extract, what indicators are there that this is a prize-winning piece?
3. Based on the extract –
   (a) Write a diary entry that Miss McDwyer makes after a day at school.

OR

   (b) Predict an ending for this short story (one or two paragraphs will suffice).
(*Junior Certificate, 2002*)

SAMPLE ANSWERS

Q1. What kind of teacher do you think Miss McDwyer is? Give reasons for your answer.

Plan

- shy
- self-conscious
- enthusiastic
- inspiring

From this extract we can see that Miss McDwyer is obviously a shy, timid person. She begins by introducing herself in a voice that was '*very low. Almost a whisper.*' She seems intimidated by the class and is very self-conscious. This is evident when she begins to speak as her words stumble over each other and she keeps tucking a curl behind her ear.

On the second day she appears to have found her feet and she is well prepared for the entrance of the students. She is '*full of enthusiasm*' for her subject and '*beamed*' at the class.

The author obviously found her to be an inspirational teacher. She opened up a sense of wonder in the students and fuels their interest in the subject. The author even states '*something ignited in me*'.

Q2. This short story was a winning entry in an under-16 national writing competition. Basing your evidence on the above extract, what indicators are there that this is a prize-winning piece?

Plan

- use of dialogue
- descriptive style
- varied syntax
- characters

This extract is very well written and these factors would indicate that it is a prize-winning short story.

The author begins with pieces of dialogue, the first tentative words spoken by the substitute teacher into the classroom. This sets the scene and reveals the innocence of Miss McDwyer at the same time. The dialogue is not over used but simply propels the story forward while developing the main characters.

The author uses a very descriptive style. The atmosphere in the classroom is created using adjectives, '*the boys' deadpan eyes brighten*'. She also uses similes throughout the piece to heighten the sense of excitement and aptly describe the feelings experienced by those in the classroom. *'They were like tigers watching their prey'. 'As if we were lost in a maze and trying to work our way out.'*

The writer uses lists of adjectives to describe the emotions felt by the student; *'yellow and purple and red, wavering and contracting, pacing and dancing.'*

The writer also varies the syntax of the piece. By varying the sentence length and structure she keeps the reader interested and allows the piece to flow. Several paragraphs end in a simple statement that provides a link to the next section, *'Something ignited in me.'* The final statement, *'after one week the paper fights began'*, punctuates the story and obviously leads on to the next section in the story.

The writer also captures the types of characters very well. The vicious schoolboys just waiting *'for the kill'*, the naïve young teacher *'full of enthusiasm'* and the world-weary student, *'what could possibly be found in a short story?'*

Each of these aspects of her writing style indicate that this is a prize-winning piece.

Q3. Based on the extract below:
(a) Write a diary entry that Miss McDwyer makes after a day at school.

OR

(b) Predict an ending for this short story.

Diary entry

Dear Diary,
Well thank God that is over. The first day in any class is always nerve wracking but today was worse than before. I started my first day as sub for Mr. Hennessy's English class. I promised myself that I would be confident and assured when I walked into the classroom, but as soon as I got there I crumbled. They just looked so intimidating. They all stared at me and I ended up stumbling over my words and fiddling with my hair. They looked like tigers eyeing up their prey!

Tomorrow will be different. I am going to be there first tomorrow and establish myself as the dominant one. I think I'll start on short stories. I like those and hopefully some of my enthusiasm will rub off. There must be one or two at least that I can reach. I think James Brown's 'Old House' would be a good place to start. It has so much symbolism that it will surely keep them interested.

OK, goodnight diary. I will need my energy for tomorrow if I am ever to win over this class. Wish me luck!

E. McDwyer

Read the following extract carefully and then answer the questions which follow. The extract (in edited form) is taken from *The Pupil* by Caro Fraser.

> **Background to the extract:**
> • **Anthony Cross** has a holiday job as a porter in Spitalfields market in London.

The Pupil

Wednesday was not going well for Anthony Cross. His day had begun at 4 a.m., and it was now nearly nine. It had been drizzling steadily since the first grey shadows of dawn had crept over the city, and the lanes and alleyways around Spitalfields market were glistening with rain and vegetable refuse. The great steel barn of the fruit market echoed with the shouts of porters, the whinings of forklift trucks, the crashing of crates and the tramp of feet.

While Anthony hauled crates and tallied sacks of onions, Mr Mant, his boss, would emerge regularly from the cracked wooden den that he called his office and shuffle across to the café with his little stainless steel teapot. There it would be filled, and Mr Mant, small and dark and bent and unwashed, would make his way back to the office with his tea and doughnut. He never offered to share his tea with Anthony.

It was the mere fact of the steady rain that made Anthony's life so miserable. Wheeling the heavy handcart, with its iron-rimmed wheels, in and out of the market, he had become drenched. There was nothing waterproof he could wear without sweating horribly, and now he could feel the damp seeping in under his jersey, through his shirt and into his skin, blotting and chilling him. The rain made the cobbles slippery, and a treacherous film of muck and rotten vegetable matter lay everywhere. Anthony's working gloves had become sodden and unmanageably heavy, forcing him to discard them, and now his hands were chafed from tiny splinters on the sides of the raw wooden pallet. Anthony pondered the dreadful possibility of spending one's entire life as a market porter. With a sigh, he turned to his final distasteful task of the morning, the disposal of five rotten bags of potatoes.

Suddenly he heard the voice of his friend Len in the distance. "Allo, Tone', Len said nonchalantly. 'Fancy some grub?'

Anthony's mouth watered at the thought of a mushroom omelette and fried bread, washed down by a large cup of hot, sweet coffee. He nodded and they set off through the rain to the café. Len's great ambition in life, ever since he had first come to work at the market at the age of sixteen, had been to drive a forklift truck. He regarded Anthony with a mix of admiration (for his obvious intelligence) and pity (for his inability to appreciate the finer things in life, such as Millwall Football Club). Their discussions were normally limited to cars and television programmes.

Len was watching Anthony speculatively as he mopped up the last of his mushroom omelette. ''Ow long more are you working 'ere, then, Tone?' Anthony looked up. 'I don't know. Not much longer. Until I finish my apprenticeship for becoming a barrister.' Len's interest slipped away from Anthony and his career, and moved on to more immediate interests. 'You fancy coming to a disco in Hackney tonight?' Anthony shook his head; he had never yet accepted one of Len's invitations, but he was touched that Len continued to issue them. 'I can't. I've got to go to see my father,' he said. And then he sighed, thinking of his father and wishing that he could go to Hackney, after all.

From *The Pupil* by Caro Fraser

QUESTIONS

1. Why does Anthony dislike his holiday job in the market so much? Support your answer by reference to the extract.
2. If you were to choose to be friendly with either Anthony *or* Len, which of the two would you choose and why? Support your answer by reference to the extract.
3. Do you think the writer of the above extract brings the London market to life? Support your answer by reference to the extract.

(Junior Certificate, 2003)

Studied Fiction

SAMPLE QUESTION

You have been asked to recommend for an award a novel or short story which you have studied. Write to the panel of judges recommending your chosen short story or novel.

(Junior Certificate, 2003)

Some of the following prompts may help you in structuring your answer:

– story and plot outline
– interesting content/theme
– characterisations
– opening/ending
– words and images
– style of writing

The novel I have studied is *To Kill a Mockingbird* by Harper Lee. I would strongly recommend this novel for an award as, on all levels, it is an excellent novel.

The story keeps your attention from beginning to end. It is told through the eyes of Scout, a young girl at the time of the events, but the adult Scout is recounting the story. This dual perspective gives us an insight into events that a purely childlike perspective could not give, while still retaining an element of authenticity and realism.

The key elements of the plot involve the trial of Tom Robinson and the children's fascination with their reclusive neighbour Boo Radley. Through Harper Lee's exploration of these two events the themes of racism and prejudice are developed. Unfortunately for Tom Robinson there is no change in his situation. His death shows how slow the rate of acceptance in the south was. However for Boo Radley the last walk home accompanied by Scout signifies a greater acceptance by those in the community of those who are different.

The way these themes are explored in the novel is one reason for its recommendation for this award. The theme of growing up is also dealt with in the novel. The fact that Tom Robinson, a cripple, is convicted of a crime he could not have committed is a turning point in the novel for Jem. He sees the corruption of the adult world and his childish innocence and innate belief in the wisdom of adults are shattered.

The key characters are accurately and vividly described. Atticus Finch is a single father trying to raise his family on his own and maintain his own standards and morals under threat from the outside world. His stand against his own neighbours outside the jailhouse, as witnessed by Scout, is a key moment of conflict in the novel. Here he physically stands up for what he believes in – the integrity of the law – and faces down all opposition. His character is central to the novel. He is Scout's hero and she looks up to him throughout the novel. Even Jem begins to resemble his father towards the end of the novel by standing up for what he believed in and protecting Scout. These key characters and these moments of conflict give the novel depth and resonance.

Harper Lee is also very descriptive. The atmosphere created on the walk home after the pageant is heightened by the blinkered vision of Scout. As the story is told from her perspective and she is inside the cumbersome costume, we the reader are limited to what she can see. The effect is very dramatic and heightens the suspense and tension when the fate of Bob Ewell is revealed.

Overall this novel deals with universal themes by exploring key events through the eyes of a child, giving us different perspectives on interesting and believable characters. Along with the very descriptive writing style these reasons are why I would like to recommend this novel for an award.

Questions on Studied Fiction

1. Choose a novel or short story you have studied where a particular mood or atmosphere is created.
   (a) Describe the mood or atmosphere.
   (b) How does the writer create this mood or atmosphere?
   Support your answer by reference or quotation.

   (Junior Certificate, 2003)

2. Select a novel or short story you have studied that deals with conflict or difficulties.
   Explain
   • How this conflict or these difficulties arose.
   • To what extent the conflict or difficulty was resolved.
   Support your answer by reference to the novel or short story.

   (Junior Certificate, 2002)

3. From a novel you have studied choose a character who made a significant impact on another person's life.
   • Outline this character's influence supporting your answer by reference to the novel.
   • Would you have liked to encounter this person in your own life? Give reasons for your answer.

   (Junior Certificate, 2002)

8
Spelling, Grammar and Punctuation

In both Papers 1 and 2, the examiner will be aware of your standard of writing. This will either allow the examiner to reward you for good use of language or penalise you for bad spelling and punctuation.

In order to write well you don't need to have long involved sentences using lots of 'big words'. You **do** need to make yourself clearly understood. A simple sentence that is well written is better than a long sentence with words that are used incorrectly. Keep it simple!

There are a few simple mistakes which are frequently made by students which are easy to rectify. Keeping an eye on these points can make all the difference.

Punctuation

Punctuation is there for a reason. It is your way of telling the reader exactly what you mean. Sloppy punctuation results in work that is difficult to follow and doesn't make sense.

The most basic element of punctuation is the full stop.

FULL STOP

You must have a full stop at the end of every sentence. If a question mark or exclamation mark is more appropriate, they serve the same function as a full stop.

You also use full stops to show that a word has been shortened or abbreviated, e.g. Mr., St.

CAPITAL LETTERS

Every new sentence must begin with a capital letter.

Capital letters are also used for the name of something:

- A person's name e.g. Lara Croft
- The name of a country or place e.g. Kildare, Ballyhaunis
- Books or film titles e.g. *Mission Impossible*
- Months e.g. January
- Rivers e.g. Shannon
- Football teams e.g. Manchester United.

COMMA

Commas are used to separate items on a list, or to divide phrases in a long sentence. A comma gives the reader an indication where to pause so that the sentence makes sense e.g.

They walk to school everyday, except Thursdays when they get a lift.

I stopped, stared, and glanced back again just to be sure.

APOSTROPHES

When in doubt students tend to either stick in apostrophes everywhere or else leave them out completely. Either option will leave the examiner trying to guess what you mean and penalising your marks. There are **two** occasions when you use an apostrophe.

1. To show that a letter is missing e.g.

   Don't   → Do not
   I'm   → I am
   You've → You are
   They're → They are

2. To show ownership e.g.

   Mary's dog
   The teacher's apple

   Do not put an apostrophe before every 's'. It is incorrect and unnecessary!

- If a word is plural (more than one) and has added an 's', e.g. boys, and you wish to show ownership, e.g. the bags belonging to the boys, then the apostrophe goes after the 's' e.g.

  → The boys' bags

Exception
As with all rules there is an exception.

   It is   →   It's

But if you want to show ownership there is no apostrophe e.g.

   The horse lost **its** shoe.

Direct Speech

In your personal writing you will probably use direct speech at some point e.g. a conversation between two characters.

   Follow these punctuation guidelines to write it correctly.
   1. Start a new line every time a new character speaks. This makes it easier for the examiner to follow who is speaking and makes sure that you remember to use quotation marks where necessary.
   2. The first word in any direct speech is always a capital letter.
   3. The quotation marks must surround the words that come out of a character's mouth.
   4. Add a comma after the quotation if followed by more writing e.g.

   'Oh hello,' said Mary.

Look at the following sample to see these guidelines at work.

'Why do we have to go today?' whined Jack, Sarah's little brother.

   'Because I said so', said Sarah, 'and I'm in charge.' She walked ahead of him down the street.

   'I'm too tired,' he tried again.

   'Hurry up or I'll leave you behind!'

   Jack rushed to catch up with his sister but her long strides soon left him straggling behind her.

DIALOGUE

When writing a dialogue you don't need to use quotation marks, but you do still need to use other appropriate punctuation. In the Personal Writing section you may choose to write your essay in this style (See Personal Writing chapter).

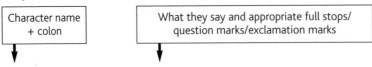

| Character name + colon | What they say and appropriate full stops/ question marks/exclamation marks |

Jack: Why do we have to go today?
Sarah: Because I said so and I am in charge.
Jack: I'm too tired.
Sarah: Hurry up or I will leave you behind!

Spelling

The following points include some of the spelling rules that seem to cause problems and a list of frequently misspelt words.

PLURALS

- For most words in plural simply add an 's' e.g.
  cars   dogs   doors   schools

- Some words are irregular and form the plural by changing a letter or letters, or by staying the same e.g.
  children   sheep

- Words that end in 'ch' add –es e.g.
  marches   churches

- Words that end in 'o' add –es e.g.
  heroes   volcanoes

  Unless there is a vowel (a, e, i, o, u) before the 'o' e.g.
  stereos   videos

  – Except the following: pianos   solos   halos

- Words that end in 'y' change to –ies e.g.
  fly   flies
  sky   skies

Unless there is a vowel before the 'y' e.g.
monkey   monkeys

- Words that end in 'x' add –es e.g.
  boxes

  Words that end in 'f' or 'fe' –change to –ves e.g.
  loaf ➔ loaves
  Except: chiefs   cliffs   griefs   roofs

Other Spelling Rules

- 'i' before 'e' except after 'c' e.g.
  th<u>ie</u>f
  rec<u>ei</u>ve

  Except: eight   either   foreign   neighbour   seizure   neither   sleigh   weird

- There/Their/They're
  There = A place or a statement e.g.
  It's over there. There are too many people here.

  Their = belonging to them e.g.
  Their bags, their coats, their hats.

  They're = They are e.g.
  They're very tired.

FREQUENTLY MISSPELT WORDS

Check the following list for words you frequently misspell.

Accept	Dissatisfied	Quiet
Awkward	Except	Quite
Beginning	Fulfil	Rough
Character	Guard	Sincerely
Choice	Mediterranean	Skilful
Choose	Naïve	Thought
Chose	Panicked	Through
Conscience	Prejudice	Tough
Conscientious	Principal	Trafficked
Conscious	Principle	Vicious
Definitely	Probably	Violent
Disappointment	Psycho	

9

Exam Papers

JUNIOR CERTIFICATE EXAMINATION, 2004

ENGLISH – HIGHER LEVEL – PAPER 1
180 marks
9.30–12.00

YOU MUST ATTEMPT ALL 4 SECTIONS

IT IS SUGGESTED THAT YOU SPEND ABOUT HALF AN HOUR ON EACH
OF SECTIONS 1, 3, 4 AND ABOUT ONE HOUR ON SECTION 2

Section 1: Reading   [40]

Read carefully the following passage and then answer the questions that follow.

'Call the usher! The pleasure of movie-going is becoming a pain, thanks to noisy, guzzling, mobile-phone-using talkers, kickers and general pests.' So said Irish Times journalist Hugh Linehan in an article in his newspaper. The article appears below in edited form.

Shhhhhhhhhh!

Maybe it's because I'm a spoiled snobbish elitist – and that's not something I'm happy about – but I have to confess I'm finding it increasingly painful to go to the movies with the rest of you, the great paying public. It's not because of the cinemas – standards of projection, sound, seating and ventilation have improved out of all recognition over the last ten years – but (and I am sorry to say this) your standards of behaviour seem to be disimproving all the time.

Kickers are a real source of irritation. The kicker problem is exacerbated by the design of modern cinema seats – a kicked seat reverberates right along the row, so that it can be nigh-well impossible to figure out where it's coming from. In the 1970s, they called this Sensurround and people paid to experience it in movies such as *Earthquake* and *Towering Inferno*. Nowadays, you can have your own personal towering inferno as you reach boiling point after two hours of bone-shaking juddering.

Up until recently, the mobile phenomenon seemed to be spinning out of control. Cinemas were buzzing like beehives with the wretched things and some buffoons even had the cheek to strike up conversations on them during the film. There will always be buffoons, but a corner seems to have been turned in recent times. Thankfully, cinemas have now taken to putting reminders on the screen telling people to switch off their phones, and many appear to be doing so. On an electronically related topic, by the way, what sort of benighted fool needs a watch that beeps on the hour, every hour?

I have some sympathy for those who feel nauseated by the smell of warm buttery popcorn which is so much a part of the multiplex experience, but it doesn't bother me that much. If people want to eat wildly overpriced, grease-saturated cardboard, then that's their business. At least popcorn has the virtue of being (almost) silent food – far better than the high-pitched crackle of the jumbo crisp packet or the extended kitchen-sink gurgle of the almost-drained Coke.

→

To my mind the real problem in cinemas these days is talkers. They're everywhere and they come in a variety of species. One kind can't help giving a blow-by-blow commentary of the movie. They're bad enough, but there is worse. Top of the list come those who just utterly ignore the film in favour of their own chat. Western society has devised countless places where people can communicate with each other, but cafes, restaurants or street corners are just not good enough for these people – apparently not when they can have the added pleasure of spoiling other people's enjoyment.

Then, there are those who think that any break in the dialogue has been inserted by the filmmaker expressly for them to start talking. The minute there is a pause of more than a couple of seconds they launch into conversation. This is not to forget the downright stupid, who spend most of the time asking questions: 'Who's she?' 'What happened there?' By the time they've got an answer they've missed the next plot point, and the whole weary rigmarole starts all over again.

What is the reason for this plague? The general decline in politeness in society may have something to do with it, but it doesn't fully explain the seemingly unstoppable desire to talk when the lights to down. We don't want funereal silence; a good comedy, horror or action movie can be immeasurably improved by the communal experience of seeing it with an audience. People can shriek or laugh to their hearts' content, and there is a real sense of a shared magical experience. After all, we're all together in the cinema . . . in the dark. And you never know who is sitting next to you!

Answer the following **three** questions:

1. Hugh Linehan outlines a number of complaints about cinemagoers' behaviour. List two examples of behaviour he finds particularly irritating. Basing your answer on the text, explain why he finds these examples irritating. (10)
2. Hugh Linehan describes himself as a 'spoiled, snobbish elitist' in the opening line of the passage. Based on what you have read, would you agree with this description? Support your answer with references to the text.   (15)
3. Basing your answer on the way the passage is written, how serious do you think the writer is in his criticism of the behaviour of cinema audiences?   (15)

Section 2: Personal Writing   [70]

Write a prose composition on any **one** of the following titles. Except where otherwise stated, you are free to write in any form you wish, e.g. narrative, descriptive, dramatic, short story, etc.

You will be rewarded for:

- A personal approach to the subject
- An appropriate style
- Liveliness and a good choice of words
- Organisation and accuracy

1. My pet hates.

2. Write a composition beginning 'Finally the smoke cleared and I could see . . .'

3. You discover that a close friend of yours has found some money. Write the conversation that takes place between you about what to do with the cash.

4. Movie magic.

5. Your Aunt and Uncle have asked you to mind their house and pets while they are on holiday. Write about your experiences while house-sitting.

6. The future: things I dread and things I look forward to.

7. Look at the picture opposite and write a composition inspired by it.

8. You are preparing to represent Ireland in a sport of your choice at the 2004 Olympic Games. Write a series of diary entries recording your preparations.

Section 3: Functional Writing   [30]

Answer **either** Question 1 **or** Question 2.

You will be rewarded for:

- Well-structured answers
- Clarity of expression
- An appropriate tone
- Good grammar, spelling, punctuation and correct use of capitals

1. Write a review for a young peoples' magazine of any book, film, computer game or concert you have recently experienced. Your answer should include an introduction, description, evaluation and recommendation.

OR

2. You feel strongly about Hugh Linehan's article in Section 1. Write a letter to the editor of the newspaper in which you outline your views in response to the article.

Section 4: Media Studies   [40]

Examine carefully the advertisement below and answer **either** Question 1 **or** Question 2.

1. (a) What elements of this advertisement contribute to its impact? Your answer should refer to at least two elements.
   (b) Who do you think the target audience for this advertisement might be? Explain your answer with reference to the advertisement.

OR

2. (a) What is the function of the editor of a newspaper?
   (b) You are the editor of your school's annual magazine. Write an editorial for the publication on any aspect of student behaviour you wish to encourage or discourage.

JUNIOR CERTIFICATE EXAMINATION, 2004

ENGLISH – HIGHER LEVEL – PAPER 2
(180 marks)
1.30–4.00

YOU MUST ATTEMPT ALL THREE SECTIONS ON THIS PAPER.

EACH SECTION CARRIES 60 MARKS.

SPEND ABOUT 45 MINUTES ON EACH SECTION.

Section 1: Drama [60]
Answer QUESTION ONE and QUESTION TWO

Question One (30)

Answer either **(A) or (B)**.

(A) SHAKESPEAREAN DRAMA

The following extract (in edited form) is taken from *The Tempest* by William Shakespeare. Read the extract carefully and then answer the questions which follow.

Background to this extract:

This scene is set on a deserted island where Prospero and his daughter Miranda, a beautiful girl of fifteen, have been living in exile for twelve years. A violent storm strikes the island. Ferdinand, son of the King of Naples, is shipwrecked and washed ashore. He believes that his father and all others on board have been drowned. Miranda and Ferdinand meet and fall in love at first sight. Prospero likes this development, but pretends otherwise in order to test their love.

Prospero: Say what thou seest yond.
Miranda: *(seeing Ferdinand for the first time)* What is't? A spirit?
Lord, how it looks about! Believe me, sir,
It carries a brave form. But 'tis a spirit.

Prospero: No daughter. It eats and sleeps and hath such senses
As we have. This youth thou seest
Was in the wreck; and, but he's somewhat stained
With grief, thou mightst call him
A goodly person. He hath lost his fellows,
And strays about to find them.

Miranda: I might call him a thing divine, for nothing natural
I ever saw so noble.

Prospero: *(Aside)* This love begins as I see it.

Ferdinand: *(Approaching Miranda)* Most sure the goddess
On whom these airs attend!
O you wonder!
Be you maid or no?

Miranda: No wonder, Sir, but certainly a maid.

Ferdinand: O! Ye gods! Such sadness, and such joy
Do mingle in my soul this day.
Ferdinand begins to weep.

Prospero: *(harshly)* Why weepst thou in such an unmanly fashion
Who are so young and strong?

Miranda: Why speaks my father so ungently? This
Is the second man that e'er I saw; the first
That e'er I sighed for. Pity move my father!

Ferdinand: *(tearfully)* I weep, who with mine eyes
Beheld the king, my father, drowned.

Miranda: Alack for mercy! O noble youth!

Ferdinand: O you wonder! If a virgin, and your affections
Not gone forth, I'll make you the Queen of Naples.

Prospero: *(Aside)* They are both in either's powers. But this swift love
I must uneasy make, lest too easy winning
Make the prize light.
(To Ferdinand, with mock severity) One word more!
Thou hast put thyself upon this island as a spy,
To win it from me, who is Lord of it.

Ferdinand: No, as I am a man!

Miranda: There's nothing bad can dwell in such a man. If . . .

Prospero: *(Interrupting her abruptly)* Follow me, traitor!
(Turns to Miranda)
Speak not you for him, he's a traitor!
(To Ferdinand)
Come!

I'll bind thy neck and feet together. Sea-water
Shalt thou drink; thy food shall be the fresh-brook mussels
Withered roots and husks wherein the acorn cradled.
Follow!

Miranda: *(Grabbing Prospero's cloak)* I beg you, Father!

Prospero: Hence! Hang not on my garments.

Miranda: Sir, have pity. I'll be his guarantor.

Prospero: Silence! One word more shall make me scold thee, if not hate thee, if not
hate thee.
What, pleading for an imposter?
Hush, foolish wench! Compared to most men, this fellow
Is a beast, and they to him are angels.

Miranda: My love is then most humble. I have no ambition to see a goodlier man.

Prospero: *(To Ferdinand)* Come! Obey!

Ferdinand: My spirits, as in a dream, are all bound up.
My father's loss, the weakness which I feel,
The wrack of all my friends and this man's threats –
Yet all are light to me
Could I but through my prison once a day,
Behold this maid.

Prospero: *(Aside)* It works.
(To Ferdinand) Come on –
Be of comfort. My father's of a better nature, sir
Than he appears by speech. This is unusual.
He speaks not like himself.

Prospero: Come, follow! *(To Miranda)* Speak not for him.

Exit all.

Answer **two** of the following questions.

1. What do we learn of the character of Ferdinand from the above extract.
2. The name Miranda means 'wonder', and Ferdinand certainly thinks that she is a wonder. What is wonderful about the growing relationship between Miranda and Ferdinand? Support your answer by reference to the text.
3. If you were directing this scene, what suggestions would you make to Prospero as to how he should play his part in order to convey his true feelings to the audience?

(B) OTHER DRAMA

The following extract (in edited form) is taken from *The Glass Menagerie* by Tennessee Williams. Read the extract carefully and answer the questions which follow.

> **Background to this extract:**
> This play is set in St Louis, USA, in the 1930s. This scene is set in the home of Amanda, a deserted wife, who lives with her daughter, Laura, and her son, Tom. Laura is an extremely shy and introverted girl. Amanda is very anxious for Laura to marry and persuades Tom to invite his colleague, Jim, to their home for dinner. Laura and Jim are left alone after dinner.

Jim: You know – you're – well – very different.
Surprisingly different from anyone else I know ... Do you mind me telling you that.
Laura is too shy to speak.

Jim: I mean it in a nice way. Has anyone ever told you that you were pretty?
Laura looks up slowly with wonder and shakes her head.

Jim: Well, you are! In a very different way from anyone else. And all the nicer for that difference too.

Laura: In what respects am I pretty?

Jim: In all respects – believe me! Your eyes – your hair – are pretty! Your hands are pretty! Laura, you know, if I had a sister like you, I'd do the same thing as Tom. I'd bring fellows home and – introduce them to her. The right type of boys – of a type to appreciate her.
Only ... Tom made a mistake about me.
Maybe I've got no call to be saying this. This may not have been the idea in having me over. But what if it was? There's nothing wrong about that. The only trouble is that in my case – I'm not in a situation to do the right thing ...
I can't take down your number and say I'll phone. I can't call up next week and – ask for a date. I thought I'd better explain the situation in case – you misunderstood it and – hurt your feelings ...
Pause. Slowly, very slowly, Laura's look changes.

Laura: *(Faintly)* You – won't – call?

Jim: No, Laura, I can't. As I was just explaining. I've got strings on me, Laura. I've been – going steady! I go out all the time with a girl named Betty ... I met her last summer on a boat trip up the river to Alton. Well, right away from the start it was – love!
Laura sways slightly forward and grips the arm of the sofa. Jim fails to notice.

Jim: Being in love has made a new man of me! The power of love is really tremendous! Love is something that changes the whole world, Laura.
He looks at her again.

Jim: It happened that Betty's aunt took sick. She had to go to Centralia. So Tom – when he asked me to dinner – I naturally accepted the invitation, not knowing that you – that he – that I –
He stops awkwardly. I wish that you would – say something.
Laura bites her lip, which was trembling, and then bravely smiles.
At this moment Amanda rushes brightly into the room bearing a jug of fruit punch.

Amanda: Well, isn't the air delightful after the shower? I've made you children a little liquid refreshment. Why, Laura! You look so serious!

Jim: We were having a serious conversation.

Amanda: Good! Now you're better acquainted!

Jim: *(Uncertainly)* Ha – ha! Yes.

Answer **two** of the following questions.
1. Jim is described as 'a nice ordinary young man'. Would you agree with this? Refer to the text in support of your answer.
2. Imagine that you are directing a production of *The Glass Menagerie*. What suggestions would you make to the actress who is playing the part of Laura? Consider, for example, body language and tone of voice.
3. Based on what you learn about Amanda from the above text, write the scene you imagine could have taken place between Amanda and Laura after Jim's departure. Use suitable dialogue and stage directions.

Question Two   (30)

Answer **EITHER 1 OR 2**

NB You must give the name of the play that you choose. You may **NOT** choose either of the scenes quoted on this examination paper as the basis for your answer.

1. Name a play you have studied in which one character rebels against another. With which character did you have more sympathy? Give reasons for your answer making reference to the play.

OR

2. Name a play you have studied. Choose a scene from this play you found either happy **or** sad. Describe how the playwright conveys this happiness **or** sadness.

Section 2: Poetry   [60]

Read the following poem by TS Eliot and answer the questions that follow.

> The winter evening settles down
> With the smell of steaks in passageways.
> Six o'clock.
> The burnt-out end of smoky days.
> And now a gusty shower wraps
> The grimy scraps
> Of withered leaves about your feet
> And newspapers from vacant lots;
> The showers beat
> On broken blinds and chimney-pots,
> And at the corner of the street
> A lonely cab-horse steams and stamps.
>
> And then the lighting of the lamps.
>
> *TS Eliot* (1888–1965)

Answer QUESTION ONE and QUESTION TWO

Question One   (30)

Answer **both** 1 **and** 2.

1. What title would you give to this poem? Explain your choice with detailed reference to the poem.
2. Do you think that this is a well-written poem? Defend your point of view with reference to the text of the poem.

Question Two   (30)

Answer **EITHER 1 OR 2**.

NB In answering you may **NOT** use the poem given. You must give the title of the poem you choose and the name of the poet.

1. Being in love has always inspired men and women to express their feelings in verse.

   Select a love poem you have studied.
   (a) Describe what happens in this poem.
   (b) How does the lover express her/his feelings?
   (c) Would you like to have this poem written for you on St Valentine's Day? Give reasons for your answer.

OR

2. It is said that every reader brings the same poem a new life. Choose a poem you have studied which has a special and very personal meaning for you.
   (a) Explain why this poem has a special meaning for you. Describe how the poet has made it possible for you, the reader, to identify with the message in this poem.
   (b) What is there in the language and imagery of the poem that attracts you?

Section 3: Fiction [60]

Read the following short story carefully and then answer the questions that follow. The story (in edited form) is called *Fear*, by Rhys Davies.

As soon as the boy into the compartment he felt there was something queer in it. The only other occupant was a slight Indian man who sat in a corner. There was also a faint sickly scent. For years afterwards, whenever he smelled that musk odour again, the terror of this afternoon came back to the boy.

He went to the other end of the compartment and sat in the opposite corner. There were no corridors in these local trains. The man smiled at him in a friendly fashion. The boy became aware of a deep vague unease, but it would look silly to jump out of the compartment now. The train began to move.

Immediately, the man began to utter a low humming chant. The hum penetrated above the noise of the train's wheels. Startled, the boy turned from staring out of the window and forced himself to glance at the man. The man was looking at him. Something coiled up in the boy. It was as if his soul took primitive fear. The humming chant continued. The musk scent was stronger. Yet, this was not all. The boy felt that some fearful thing lurked in the compartment, a secret power of something evil.

Abruptly, the compartment was plunged into darkness as the train entered a tunnel. The boy crouched. He knew that the man's eyes were gazing at him. What was this strange presence of evil in the air, stronger now in the dark?   →

Suddenly, daylight came crashing into the compartment. The boy stared dully at the man. He saw the man's lips part in a full enticing smile. 'You not like dark tunnels?' The smile continued seductively as flecks of light danced wickedly in his eyes.

'Come!' he beckoned with a long finger. The boy did not move. 'You like pomegranates?'* He took from the luggage rack a brown basket, crossing over and sat down beside the boy. 'Nice pomegranates,' he smiled with good humour.

The boy was aware of the sickly perfume beside him and of a presence that was utterly alien. The man, still humming, lifted the basket's lid. There was no glow of gleaming fruits. But from the basket's depth rose the head of a snake, swaying towards the man's lips. It was a cobra.

Something happened to the boy, some primitive warning. He leaped and flung himself across the compartment. He gave a sharp shriek. But his eyes could not tear themselves from that reared head. Somehow, the boy knew that he had evoked rage. The cobra was writhing in anger. More fearful was the dilation of the throat, its skin swelling evilly into a hood. The boy sensed the destructive fury of the hood. He became very still. The man did not stop humming. The snake was pacified. Its head ceased to lunge and its body sank back into the basket. The man closed the basket and fastened it securely. Then, he turned angrily to the boy, making a contemptuous sound. 'I show you cobra and you jump and shout, heh! Make him angry. I give you free performance with cobra and you jump and scream. I sing to keep cobra quiet in train. Cobra not like train! Not liking you jump up and shout.

The boy was not stirred.

The train was drawing into a station, not the boy's station, but he made a sudden blind leap, opened the door, saw it was not the platform side, but he jumped. He ran up the track and dived under some wire railings, like a hare that knows its life is precarious among the colossal dangers of the world.

* Tropical fruit

Answer QUESTION ONE and QUESTION TWO

Question One

Answer **two** of the following questions.
1. Do you find the boy's reaction to the snake and the Indian snake charmer normal or exaggerated? Give reasons for your answer.

2. 'We enjoy reading stories like this one because they enable us to explore the outer edges of the unknown, strangeness, things that cannot be explained – without feeling any danger to ourselves.' Do you agree with this statement? Why? Why not? Support your answer with reference to the story.
3. The title of this story is *Fear*. In your opinion, is the writer successful in conveying a sense of the boy's fear to the reader? Give reasons for your opinion and support your answer by reference to the text.

Question Two

Answer **EITHER 1 OR 2.**

NB In answer you may **not** use the extract given above as the basis for your answer. You must give the title of the text you choose and the name of the author.

1. Many novels or short stories show the conflict between good and evil. Name a novel <u>or</u> short story you have studied where there is conflict between good and evil. Trace how the author presents this conflict.

OR

2. Choose a novel <u>or</u> a short story you have studied which contains a strong element of surprise.

   (a) Describe the setting of the novel or short story.
   (b) Describe the events leading up to the surprise in this novel or short story.
   (c) How did the surprise in the novel or short story affect one or more of the characters?